Caroline O'Connor

August - 2009

THE REAL STARS

ALSO BY BEN STEIN

HOW SUCCESSFUL PEOPLE WIN:
Using "Bunkhouse Logic" to Get What You Want in Life

HOW TO RUIN YOUR FINANCIAL LIFE

HOW TO RUIN YOUR LIFE (hardcover)
(also available as an audio book)

HOW TO RUIN YOUR LOVE LIFE

HOW TO RUIN YOUR LIFE
tradepaper (comprises the three titles above)

HOW YOU CAN SELL ANYONE ANYTHING
(co-written with Barron Thomas) (available May 2008)

26 STEPS TO SUCCEED IN HOLLYWOOD . . . or Any Other Business
(co-written with Al Burton)

ALSO BY BEN STEIN AND PHIL DEMUTH

CAN AMERICA SURVIVE?:
The Rage of the Left, the Truth, and What to Do about It

YES, YOU CAN BE A SUCCESSFUL INCOME INVESTOR!:
Reaching for Yield in Today's Market

YES, YOU CAN GET A FINANCIAL LIFE!:
Your Lifetime Guide to Financial Planning

YES, YOU CAN STILL RETIRE COMFORTABLY!:
The Baby-Boom Retirement Crisis and How to Beat It

THE REAL STARS

In Today's America,
Who Are the True Heroes?

BEN STEIN

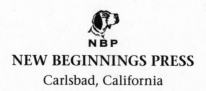

NBP

NEW BEGINNINGS PRESS
Carlsbad, California

ISBN: 978-1-4019-1144-7

Printed in the United States of America

*For every man
and woman who
wears the uniform and
risks life itself for freedom
and for every member of
their families. Words are not
enough. We owe them
everything.*

CONTENTS

PREFACE

IT'S CHRISTMASTIME. In Beverly Hills, where my wife and I live, the streets have stupendous Christmas displays of Baccarat crystals hanging above the intersections. The stores are jammed with shoppers buying jewels, furs, Bentleys, trips to Fiji for the holidays. Near Palm Springs, in Rancho Mirage, where we spend time, the stores are showing elegant champagne glasses, thick gold bracelets, alligator purses that start at $5,000. The rage there among the wealthy is to have one's own jet. In fact, you're nobody without a plane of some kind. This makes me a nobody, but the skies above Palm Springs are filled with private jets of the somebodies coming in for the holidays.

In New York City, Fifth Avenue is afire with lights from Saks Fifth Avenue, Tiffany's, Henri Bendel. The shoppers are laughing, gossiping into their cell phones. After a long day of shopping, the men and women have $22 martinis, $50 champagne flutes, and $45 rib-eye-steak entrées. Laughter, laughter, laughter, everywhere. The stock market is hitting new highs. Everyone is rich, it seems.

On Fisher Island, Florida, the yachtsmen gather and tell of how there are waiting lists for $70 million 200-foot yachts with saloons that are 75 feet long.

Each boat comes with five smaller boats in its belly and a gourmet kitchen.

The owners talk of deals and more deals and how long it will be until they are billionaires. Their wives giggle and show off how thin they are because you can never be too thin or too rich.

In Mosul and Kirkuk and Fallujah, in Forward Operating Base Warhorse near Baghdad, in tents and in corrugated-steel boxes that serve as barracks, men and women in the uniforms of the United States—Marine, Army, Navy, Air Force, National Guard—sweat and sleep and prepare to go and fight and die and bleed. They risk their lives every single day. In Afghanistan, military men and women patrol ghostly, ghastly valleys and rural roads, waiting for a land mine or rocket attack that will lead like clockwork to an Army car or a Marine car or a Navy car or an Air Force car pulling up at their wife's front door, which an officer will knock on with some terrible news. They get paid essentially nothing.

The people in the cafés in New York don't know the people in Khost, Afghanistan, on patrol against the Taliban. The people in the Gulfstreams at Palm Springs airport don't know the men and women in the Bradleys going down alleys in Baghdad awaiting a thousand-pound bomb buried under the packed earth. The people buying Bentleys in Beverly Hills don't know the military wives who will never see their husbands again or feel their touch. If you ask the wealthy about the men in battle dress uniforms, they act embarrassed. The subject quickly changes. It's mortifying to be so goddamned selfish when other people are dying for you. It's like being caught naked with the maid in the laundry room: It's not supposed to be brought up.

But it *has* to be brought up. Three hundred million people are being protected by men and women they don't know. The men and women doing the huge deals on Wall Street, the men and women making millions in Hollywood, the men who cannot bear that their yacht is late being delivered, the men and women who cannot wait to read more about Lindsay Lohan, the teenagers who think they have it tough because they have to do math homework before they can play computer games, and the politicians in their neat suits—every one of us—is protected by the blood of the men and women in uniform . . . and we're ignoring their very existence.

Part of this is the way it's always been, of course. Some die that others may live. But what's new, and what's so insane, is that instead of a nation united behind these men and women in combat, solid like a rock behind their families, we pretend they don't exist. We pretend that the wars aren't happening and that what's real is what's in *People*. This is just not right. It's insulting to the men and women who offer up their lives for less than a Hollywood producer spends on tickets for parking in handicapped zones.

To me, it is amazing, incredible, magnificent, and fantastic that men will sign up to die for people they don't know. It is breathtaking that women will spend years or a lifetime serving the country that pretends they don't exist. It amazes me, whether the men and women offering up their blood are in the military or the police or the fire departments. It is a screaming miracle. There should be a beacon of thanks shrieking into the sky every second, coming from our hearts and souls. I feel as if our whole nation should be pouring out our hearts in gratitude every day and every night. We're not doing it, and this book is a small attempt, a tiny attempt, to right the balance—to talk about how insignificant, how negligible, how silly our lives are compared with the lives and deaths of the men and women who wear the uniform.

We cannot all be brave enough to do what they do. We cannot be young enough or strong enough. However, every one of us can pray and every one of us can be on our knees with gratitude. That and a few other smaller items are what this book is about.

God bless those sacred souls in their uniforms and in their hospital beds and in their graves—and the military wives and children, the marrow in the backbone of America. God bless those whose fear and courage lets us live in the lavishness and foolishness that is our daily lives.

THE
REAL
STARS

AS I BEGIN to write this, I "slug" it, as we writers say, which means I put a heading on it to identify it. This heading is "eonlineFINAL," and it gives me a shiver to write it. It has been so long that I have been doing it that I really cannot even recall when I started. Lew Harris, who founded this great site, asked me to do it maybe seven or eight years ago, and I loved doing it so much for so long, I got to believe it would never end.

But, again, all things must pass, and my column for E! Online must pass. In a way, it is a perfect time for it to pass. Lew, whom I have known forever, was impressed that I knew so many stars at Morton's [restaurant in Beverly Hills] on Monday nights. He could not get over it, in fact. So he said I should write a column about the stars I saw at Morton's and what they had to say.

It worked well for a long time, but gradually, my changing as a person and the world's change has overtaken it. On a small scale, Morton's, while better than ever, no longer attracts as many stars as it used to. It still attracts rich people in droves, and some stars (I just saw Samuel L. Jackson there a few days ago and we had a nice visit, and right before that I saw and had a splendid talk with Warren Beatty in an elevator, in which we all agreed that *Splendor in the Grass* was a super movie). But it is not the star galaxy it once was, though it probably will be again.

But there is a bigger change that has happened. I no longer think Hollywood stars are terribly important. They are uniformly pleasant, friendly people, and they treat me better than I deserve to be treated. But a man or woman who makes a huge wage for memorizing lines and reciting them in front of a camera is no longer my idea of a bright, shining star we should all look up to. How can a man or woman who makes an eight-figure wage and lives in insane luxury really be a star in today's world, if by a "star," we mean someone bright and powerful and attractive as a role model?

The real stars are not riding around in the backs of limousines or in Porsches or getting trained in yoga or

Pilates and eating only raw fruit while they have Vietnamese girls do their nails. They can be interesting, nice people, but they are not stars to me any longer.

The real star is the soldier of the 4th Infantry Division who poked his head into a hole on a farm near Tikrit, Iraq, last Saturday. He could have been met by a bomb or a hail of AK-47 bullets. Instead, he was met by an abject Saddam Hussein and the gratitude of all of the decent people of the world. The real star is the U.S. soldier who was sent to disarm a bomb next to the road north of Baghdad. He approached it and the bomb went off and killed him. A real star, the kind who haunts my memory night and day, is the U.S. soldier in Baghdad who saw a little girl playing with a piece of unexploded ordnance on a street near where he was guarding a station. He pushed her aside and threw himself on it just as it exploded. He left a desolate family in California and left a little girl alive in Baghdad.

The stars who deserve media attention are not the ones who have lavish weddings on TV, but the ones who patrol the streets of Mosul even after two of their buddies were murdered and their bodies battered and stripped for the sin of trying to protect Iraqis from terrorists. We put couples with incomes of $100 million a year on the covers of our magazines. The noncoms and officers who barely scrape by on military pay but who guard the nation in Afghanistan and Iraq and on ships and in submarines and near the Arctic Circle are anonymous as they live and as they die. I am no longer comfortable being a part of the system that has such poor values, and I do not want to perpetuate them by making believe that who is eating at Morton's is a big subject.

There are plenty of other stars in the American firmament. The police men and women who go off on patrol in South Central and have no idea if they will return alive. The orderlies and paramedics who bring in people who have been in terrible accidents and prepare them for surgery. The teachers and nurses who throw their whole spirits into caring for autistic children. The kind men and women who work in hospices and in cancer wards . . . all of these are stars, and so are the teachers and social workers who cast their mortal spans into the struggle to make something of our troubled youth. Or, think of each and every fireman who was running up the stairs at the World Trade Center to rescue men and women coming down as the towers collapsed, and you have my idea of a star.

Now, last week I told you a few of the rules I had learned to keep my sanity, and now I am going to just say a few more to help you keep your sanity and keep you in the running for stardom. The main one is that we are puny, insignificant creatures. We live as God directs that we live. We are not responsible for the operation of the universe, and what happens to us is not terribly important. God is real, not a fiction, but real—and when we turn over our lives to Him, He takes far better care of us than we could ever do for ourselves. In a word, we make ourselves *sane* when we fire ourselves as the directors of the movie of our lives and allow God to be the director. When we trust in God instead of in our own frail selves, we triumph; and when we try to control events, we suffer. When we try to do God's will, we are stars. When we do our own will, it is pathetic.

Or, I can put it another way. Years ago, I realized I could never be as great an actor as Olivier, or even close . . . or as good a comic as Steve Martin or Martin Mull or Fred Willard, or even close . . . or as good an economist as Samuelson or Friedman, or even close . . . or as good a writer as Fitzgerald, or even remotely close. But I could be a devoted father to my son and husband to my wife and, above all, a good son to the parents who had done so much for me. And this became my main task in life. I did it moderately well with my son and pretty well with my wife, but well indeed with my parents (with my sister's help). I cared for them and paid attention to them in their declining years. I stayed with my father (and my sister did, too) as he got sick, went *in extremis,* and then into a coma—and then entered immortality with my sister and me reading him the Psalms. And this was the only point at which my life touches the lives of the soldiers in Iraq or the firefighters in New York. I came to realize that life lived to help others is the only life that matters, and that it is my duty, in return for the lavish life that God has devolved upon me, to help others God has placed in my path. This is my highest and best use as a human.

As so many of you know, I am an avid Bush fan and a Republican. But I think that the best guidance on living my life I ever got was from the inauguration speech of John F. Kennedy, a Democrat, in January of 1961. On a very cold and bright day in Washington, he said words that should be the wisdom that can make any of us into stars: "With a good conscience our only sure reward, with history the final judge of our deeds, let us go forth . . . asking His blessing and His help, but knowing that here on Earth, God's work must truly be our own." Or, as I like to say, the work that we ask God to do is the work He asks us to do.

And then to paraphrase my favorite President, my boss and friend Richard Nixon, when he left the White House in August of 1974, with me standing a few feet away, "This is not good-bye. The French have a word for it: 'Au revoir.' We'll see you again."

Au revoir and thank you for reading me for so long. God bless every one of you. We'll see you again.

Monday Night at Morton's
12/20/2003

NICK & JESSICA

HEREWITH AT THIS HAPPY TIME of year, a few confessions from my beating heart:

I have no freaking clue who Nick and Jessica are. I see them on the cover of *People* and *Us* constantly when I am buying my dog biscuits and kitty litter. I often ask the checkers at the grocery stores. They never know who Nick and Jessica are, either. Who are they? Will it change my life if I know who they are and why they have broken up? Why are they so important? I don't know who Lindsay Lohan is, either, and I do not care at all about Tom Cruise's wife.

Am I going to be called before a Senate committee and asked if I am a subversive? Maybe, but I just have no clue who Nick and Jessica are. Is this what it means to be no longer young? It's not so bad.

Next confession: I am a Jew, and every single one of my ancestors was Jewish. And it does not bother me even a little bit when people call those beautiful lit-up, bejeweled trees "Christmas trees." I don't feel threatened. I don't feel discriminated against. That's what they are: Christmas trees. It doesn't bother me a bit when people say "Merry Christmas" to me. I don't think they are slighting me or getting ready to put me in a ghetto. In fact, I kind of like it. It shows that we are all brothers and sisters celebrating this happy time of year. It doesn't bother me at all that there is a manger scene on display at a key intersection near my beach house in Malibu. If people want a crèche, it's just as fine with me as is the menorah a few hundred yards away.

I don't like getting pushed around for being a Jew, and I don't think Christians like getting pushed around for being Christians. I think people who believe in God are sick and tired of getting pushed around, period. I have no idea where the concept came from that America is an explicitly atheist country. I can't find it in the Constitution, and I don't like it being shoved down my throat.

Or maybe I can put it another way: Where did the idea come from that we should worship Nick and Jessica and we aren't allowed to worship God as we understand Him?

I guess that's a sign that I'm getting old, too. But there are a lot of us who are wondering where Nick and Jessica came from and where the America we knew went to.

CBS News Sunday Morning
12/18/2005

AMERICA!

HERE IT IS Monday morning and I am out in Rancho Mirage in the heat wave. It's not really bad at all in my house. I have the curtains lowered and the air-conditioning on, and it's fine. I did have a bit of a problem earlier: My new Cadillac starts without a key. It has something called a "fob," and with that in my pocket, I can just press a button and the car starts, jumps hoops, spits out nickels, et cetera.

But somehow I mislaid one of my fobs, so I had to get new ones, and that was a bit of pain in this hot weather. Plus, my pool is really too warm to be comfortable. So that's another problem.

And then I sat down to eat my grapefruit at the table and opened yesterday's *New York Times Book Review,* and reality slapped me in the face the way it does and it should.

On the cover was the beginning of a breathtakingly horrifying review of a book about the pogroms against Polish Jews after World War II, after the defeat of the Third Reich. Jews rounded up by police, by Boy Scouts, and beaten to death with iron bars. Jews thrown off trains. Jews murdered by anyone who cared to, just in case the Jews did not get the point about how welcome they were in Poland. That could well have been my life and my death.

Then I turned the page and there was a lengthy, if confusing, review of a book about Brian Wilson and the Beach Boys. How it brought back my youth spent listening to "409," "Be True to Your School," and the dozens of other great Beach Boys songs. That was my life. Not being bashed to death with an iron bar by a Polish policeman. Not straggling back from a concentration/death camp to be taunted, "So, Stein, you're still alive," which meant that I would not be alive for long, of course. No, my younger life was riding around in a V-8 1962 Impala that I talked my pop into buying for me, and having crushes on girls who did not like me.

Why? Because of America. Because, as Philip Roth so brilliantly puts it, I live in America the way I live in my skin.

And who made it possible? The nation that armed and fought the Nazis and the Japanese, that ran into Nazi machine-gun fire at Omaha Beach to liberate France, that fought some of the worst fighting in history in the Huertgen Forest, that charged into Japanese Nambu bullets on Okinawa to beat the emperor, that sent its best and brightest to fight the battles that saved the world from a thousand-year reign of darkness.

And who still makes it possible for me to have as my main concern the keyless starters on my car? Or the heat today? Who makes it possible? The guy who faces worse heat than this every day with body armor and no air-conditioning and brutal killers laying explosives for him and sniping at him—and her—at every turn. It is impossible to go out in this heat here in Rancho Mirage. But our soldiers and Marines and Seals and Air Force people do it every day while getting shot at.

God bless this glorious American military, every wife, every child, every parent; and endless prayers for them to return home safe, mission accomplished. God bless them every moment of every day for keeping safe this America, inside of which we live as powerfully as we live in our skin. This has to be the central fact of our lives: gratitude for the men and women who make this great life possible, who wear the uniform and cover it with glory.

The American Spectator
7/26/2006

13

This Is the Civil, Good-Natured America of a Frank Capra Movie

YOU WILL NEVER GUESS where I am tonight. It's a Tuesday—not a Monday—and I'm in Philadelphia at the First Union/Comcast Center, where the GOP 2000 Convention is going on all around me.

Not only that, but I am making my way to the Bush-family box at said convention. I am being led by a pack of men in suits (some obviously packing heat) down hallways, up stairs, into elevators, and between rows of seats until finally I come to the Bush-family box.

At first, the only Bushies in it are some young grand-children of George and Barbara's—fresh and eager-looking boys and girls. Then some good-looking young people from Texas who are longtime Bush-family pals arrive.

I sit next to a young woman of 24 who puts togeth-er oil-and-gas drilling partnerships (very much like my cousin Jeffrey used to do). We talk amiably, and then in walks Mrs. Barbara Bush, looking lovely with her flash-ing blue eyes.

She walks down a row and sits next to me. The flash-bulbs and cameras go off like mad. And there is little me—who can't get to sleep most nights, who can't make his son do his homework, and who generally can't do anything.

Mrs. Bush is kind enough to recognize me right away (although, just to be sure, I tell her who I am). She immediately expresses hand-holding condolences about my father and mother, who knew the Bushes for many years. She and I then start to talk about mutual friends from the Nixon days.

I'm not going to be a cad and tell what she says. I *will* say she sums up the essence of each friend in relation to the Bushes—and to the Steins—extremely succinctly. She is smart, complimentary, and precise.

I share my M&M's and LifeSavers with her and the rest of the people in the vicinity. She is so polite. She says red LifeSavers are her favorite. I wish she were my mother.

Then President Bush comes in. By a little bit of magic, he sits next to me, and Mrs. Bush moves one seat to the left. He also expresses condolences about my father and mother.

Mr. Bush and I also talk about various friends. (He does not care to have any M&M's.) I tell Mr. and Mrs. Bush that if the achievements of the children are the measure of the parents, they are the most successful parents of the last 100 years.

Mrs. Bush looks pleased, but President Bush just smiles and brushes it off. He is a gentleman of the old school, which does not believe in excessively flattering comments. He tells me he loves my show and that I am his hero for wearing such comfortable shoes as Simples, which are my staple on the show and here at the convention.

I don't think I will share what else we talk about. But he's a polite fellow—a gentleman of astonishing modesty and lack of self-promotion, a sort of vanishing breed.

I am sorry I do not get to see President Ford, whom I also knew, but he is in the hospital with a minor cerebral incident—another vanishing breed.

After about an hour, I am ushered to another location in the convention—this time the skybox of the campaign strategist, Karl Rove. He reminds me that we met in 1978, when my dear friend Peter M. Flanigan (a real gentleman of the old school) sent me to meet Mr. Bush at a speech at Claremont College.

What a memory this man has. I then recall that I had written complimentarily about Mr. Bush, and the Reagan people were angry at me about it. Well, lots of water under the bridge since then.

All around me are young interns and assistants—boys and girls, young men and women, white, black, Asian, Latino, mostly straight, but definitely some gay. All are well dressed, very polite, and usually calling me "sir." No mean words. No sneering. No showing off connections.

I am suddenly struck by a thought: *This is how America is supposed to be. This is the civil, good-natured America of a Frank Capra movie. This is the America we sing about when we sing "America the Beautiful."*

I love it here. I am sure that Democrats feel the same about their convention and their young people. But at this convention, especially tonight, I really feel as if I were in America—the way it's supposed to be. Rarely do I get to feel this way, and it is a great feeling.

Later, I go to a **Voter.com** party on a yacht. It's being run partly by my longtime friend Carl Bernstein, the famous journalist. It is a nice party—but too hot and humid. I want to be back in the convention where everything works right. And I want Mrs. Bush to be my mother. I want them both to be my parents right now.

Small wonder GW is so self-confident, with his mom and dad.

Monday Night at Morton's
8/9/2000

THE COST OF THE WAR ON TERRORISM

ON THE SATURDAY NIGHT before Memorial Day, the cost of the war on terrorism were wearing red T-shirts. They were in a small ballroom on the second floor of the Crystal City Doubletree Hotel in northern Virginia, within sight of the Pentagon.

There were about 250 of them: children of men and women who had been killed in the fighting in Iraq and Afghanistan and in training. They were maybe from ages 5 to 15. They were handsome. They were pretty. They were cute. They had haunted eyes, some of them,

21

and some of them cried. One family had five kids, and the oldest, a beautiful 15-year-old girl, could not stop crying.

They were being watched over by about 30 mentors, who were good-looking men and women from the Air Force, Navy, Marines, and Army Honor Guard at Arlington National Cemetery. They serve as mentors and guides for the kids as the kids mourn their loss.

The kids had just gotten back from a field trip and were in a giddy, but still haunted, mood as they ate pizza. I spoke to them, hugged them, smeared my tears away as I could. I told them how pretty they were if they were girls, and how brave and handsome they looked if they were boys.

A spectacularly cute little redheaded girl named Dawn slithered around me and pretended to be a dog to be patted. Or is it petted?

I told the kids their parents had died to save this country, to give kids in Iraq and Afghanistan the chance to choose their lives and to have the freedoms we take for granted. I told them there were not enough words in the English language to thank them enough for what they had done, for the sacrifice they had made. I told them their fathers and mothers had died doing God's work.

Then I signed autographs, mostly on the kids' T-shirts, for about an hour.

I wish I were eloquent enough to tell you how brave these kids were and what a price they are paying. To lose a father while the rest of us complain about taxes and the stock market and the price of real estate. Quite a sight. Quite a concept.

How can we possibly repay them? How conceivably? There is nothing we can do but be grateful and keep them in our hearts forever.

I walked with my friend Marina Malenic, ace in WMD, to a far larger ballroom, where the widows, mothers and fathers, fiancées, widowers maybe, of the men and women who were killed were gathered.

I sat with the head of the great organization Tragedy Assistance Program for Survivors, Bonnie Carroll, who conceived of TAPS when her AF-general husband was killed in training in Alaska many years ago. Maybe it was 1998. She is a pretty, extremely smart woman, with a heart as big as a Cadillac. We sat also with several women who had lost their husbands. They were all brave—all sharing their experience, strength, and hope with each other. One woman next to me said I did not need to feel sorry for her on the death of her husband in the Mosul bombing. "I got to live with him for 22 years," she said. "I was blessed."

Everyone there wore a button with a photo of the man who had died. The men looked impossibly healthy, fit, optimistic. They could not possibly be dead, and yet they were.

Several wives spoke of their last talks with their husbands, about what it was like when the chaplain came up the driveway. Some read letters from their husbands talking about how happy they were to be helping the Iraqi children.

Bonnie spoke, perhaps the most moving speech I have ever heard in person, a difficult act to follow. She used to work with Reagan, and maybe that explains her amazing ability to get in touch with truth.

Then I spoke and gave a little talk about how we could live without the stock market, could get on without Hollywood or new cars, but could not last a week without our armed forces, and the armed forces could not last a week without the military family. "To most," I said, "the war on terrorism is an abstraction. But there is blood all over this room."

They gave me one standing ovation after another, and I left the stage dizzy with gratitude. These women—overwhelmingly women—are paying a fearful price so the rest of us can get on with our daily selfishness and greed without hindrance.

So that the witches of Beverly Hills and Fifth Avenue can go on with their shopping, these women lost their husbands. Mothers and fathers were there, too. One came up to me, a crusty couple, husband a Marine, and showed me a dollar bill from his late son's wallet when the son was killed in Iraq. The edges were covered in blood.

How can we thank these families? How can we possibly praise enough the sacrifice they and their husbands have made? How can it ever be enough?

Yet, they have something the rest of us rarely have: meaning. They know why God put them on Earth, why they live and suffer. They never doubt their worth.

Bonnie drove Marina and me back to the Watergate. I felt as if I had been with the finest people on Earth that night, the ones in God's image.

Mostly, I see the dregs of human selfishness. When I am around the military—the Honor Guard, the families, the kids, the parents, the ones who are the thin line between life and death for freedom, the ones who make our lives worth living—I have hope for the human spirit. The best of the human spirit is alive and well inside those red T-shirts.

The American Spectator Online
6/6/2005

THE HANDMAIDEN OF ALL THIS MONEY IS FEAR OF WHAT HAPPENS IF IT GOES AWAY

AND NOW, FOR A LITTLE LOOK at how Hollywood works. . . .

It begins not at Morton's but at Aquarelle, a lovely restaurant in the Watergate Hotel in Washington, D.C. Aquarelle (or "watercolor" *en anglais*) has big bay windows overlooking the Potomac. Today, the weather is a bit overcast, and the room is full of worried-looking people. The reason they look so worried is most of them are from the community of international bankers. There are big banking meetings here, and the nutcase community has been threatening giant demonstrations.

I passed a sign on a bridge near the Potomac yesterday that read: "Spill the bankers' blood in the Potomac River."

At the table next to us are about ten men and women —including the former head of the World Bank, former president of Ford Motors, and architect of the U.S. disaster in Vietnam, Robert McNamara.

I happen to dislike him, because after he got us into Vietnam when he was Secretary of Defense under Johnson, he blasted Nixon for not getting us out fast enough.

About ten feet from us is a table of black men and women who are seated with a guy who looks to me like Dick Gregory. They're all wearing big buttons with slogans against the bankers. One of them smiles at me.

Hey, it's—well, I won't tell you who it is, but it's someone I know whom I'll call Leilani. She's an attractive woman of about 45. Last time I saw her, she was a high official at a production company that makes both features and movies of the week.

I recall that she stopped at our table about two years ago and gossiped with a woman friend and told her that she, Leilani, was now making a million bucks a year, something her father, a minister, would have thought inconceivable.

"What are you doing here?" I ask.

She excuses herself to come over to my table, where I have been lunching alone. "You know I had that job that paid a million dollars a year for five years," she says, sampling my whitefish. "I lived like a queen. House in Beverly Hills. House in Santa Barbara. One of the first black people in Montecito. Three cars. First-class travel everywhere.

"Then one day, a bigger company bought our company. They were all smiles and told us we'd all be kept on. Three months later, every one of us was gone. I got a hundred thousand of severance."

"So? You're a hotshot. Where did you land?"

"Nowhere," she says. "My agents told me they could get me a job anywhere in town. They said I'd make $2 million a year in 2000. They said every studio would beg for me. I kept on spending. I had $400,000 saved. I went through it in six months. I think I spent more, not less, after I lost my job. Now it's gone. You know where I finally got a job? At a foundation trying to get more minorities into Hollywood."

"Well, that sounds all right."

"Except it only pays $110,000. I sold the house. I sold the place in Montecito. I had such big mortgages, I barely came out with a dime. Now I live in an apartment in West Hollywood. I drive a seven-year-old Acura. And I hate it."

"Is it a black *thang?*" I ask her.

"Not at all. It's a middle-aged, 'no one wants you when you're over 40 in Hollywood' thang. It's a 'getting trapped in the Velvet Alley' thang. I was crazy not to save more money. I was crazy to show off. For what?"

"'Cuz everyone else does," I say helpfully.

"And you know what? A lot of them can't sleep at night when they lose their jobs, because high-paying jobs in Hollywood are just about impossible to replace if you're not young and wired. You get it, you spend it, and then it's gone and you feel like crap."

"Maybe you'll enjoy a simpler life," I say.

"Would *you?*" she asks with a tight smile.

Oh, please, God, I think, *I don't want to find out.* I've been down that route, and I don't want to go down it again. I have seen it happen to friend after friend who was raking it in and stopped raking it in and went into a permanent sorrow and cramp.

The handmaiden of all of this money and extravagance is fear about what happens if it goes away.

The real story of Hollywood: fear.

Monday Night at Morton's
4/26/2000

BEING A STAR WOULD NOT HAVE STOPPED A BULLET

NO, I AM NOT AT MORTON'S. Far from it. I am cowering in my bed at my apartment at the Shoreham Towers in L.A., just terrified and humbly relieved at the same time. My 12-year-old son, Tommy, is sleeping next to me. May I tell you about it?

Today, we worked an insanely long day on *Win Ben Stein's Money*. Not only are we taping four shows per day, which is a killing schedule, but we are also auditioning for a cohost. The great Jimmy Kimmel is going away to work on his own fine projects, so we must find someone new.

After the audition, I went to my apartment—which I mostly use as an office—and got my mail, then filed some papers. I then drove to our new house, La Money Pit, in the heart of Beverly Hills. I felt unbelievably, awesomely tired as I drove along the empty streets, past the mansions where we do not belong. I felt like I was in a pit of fatigue.

I pulled into the alley behind our house, then into our garage. A motion-sensitive light switched on, and I got out. I walked around to the passenger side to take my heavy briefcase from the car floor. As I did, I saw two men casually walk into my garage, looking quite confident and relaxed.

I assumed they were part of the army of workmen who are endlessly toiling on our house. That was, until one of them produced an immense automatic pistol, maybe a Glock or a SIG, and pointed it at me.

This is an armed robbery! I am scared!

"Give me your money," said the man with the gun.

"Here it is," I said, as calmly as I could. I took out my wallet, filled mostly with credit cards and photos of my son, and handed it to the gunman.

"Look down," the man said. "Don't look at me."

I looked down, to where he held the huge pistol.

"Give me your watch," he said. I took off my Seiko and handed it to him.

"Give me your money," he said.

"I just did," I said, very politely.

"The rest of it," he demanded.

"I did give you all of it," I said.

The man put his hand in my jacket pockets and rummaged around. "Do you want the car?" I asked. "It's a great car. Here are the keys."

The man knocked the keys out of my hand, and they dropped to the cement floor of the garage.

God, I prayed silently, *please don't let them kill me now. Please let me see my son again.*

"What's in that?" the man with the gun asked, pointing at my ancient briefcase.

"Papers and medicines," I said, and opened it. "Do you want it? It's yours." I was shaking. My voice was breaking. I held the case in front of the man with the gun.

The man ignored it. "Give me your money," he said.

"I gave you all of it," I said. "Do you want the car?"

"Get in the car," the man said, and looked forward.

Oh, please don't let him shoot me now, I prayed to myself.

I got in the car and heard them walk away. I waited a moment and then walked into our house.

"Alex," I said to my wife, "I've just been robbed at gunpoint in our garage."

My wife and son streaked downstairs. I called 911.

I was still terrified, but my voice was not breaking any longer.

The police arrived in about one minute—maybe ten of them in several cars. They took a report. They shined flashlights up in the trees on my lawn, as if the thieves might have climbed up there to hide. They struck poses to show how muscular they were.

One of the officers studied the tile in our kitchen carefully, the tile that cost more than a car.

"I love what you've done with this tile," the cop said. "I like responding to calls in this end of Beverly Hills," he added. "I always get decorating tips. I like the way you've harmonized the countertops with the floor tile."

"Happy to help," I said.

My son said he was worried and wanted to sleep at our apartment, with its ace security.

My wife said she was not worried in the slightest and would stay at home.

Tommy and I came to the Shoreham Towers. He lay next to me, listened to a tape, and fell asleep. I cannot sleep. That's the closest to death I have been, I suspect. Anyway, it was terrifying.

Is *this* why I moved to Beverly Hills? To lose my Puppy-Wuppy? To go broke paying for custom tiles? To get robbed at gunpoint? I liked the Hollywood Hills a lot more.

Where did the robbers come from? How did they know I'd be there? Were they stalking me? Stalking my wife? Did they follow my car? Were they just lurking for hours?

I do not like this at all. Being a star would not have stopped a bullet.

Thank You, dear God, for letting me live another day to be with my boy.

I look out the immense windows of my apartment at the yellowish white lights of the city against the gray-black haze of Los Angeles by night. There's too much going on here.

Monday Night at Morton's
1/12/2000

NIXON

RICHARD NIXON. Let's start with my connection with him. In 1952, when I was seven years old, I read an official campaign biography of Ike and Dick passed out in school by the Montgomery County Republican Committee. Only one fact from that document lingers in my mind: When Richard Nixon was a young man, he met and fell madly in love with Patricia Ryan. Alas, Pat Ryan was already going with someone else. But Richard Nixon would not take no for an answer. He insisted on sitting on Pat Ryan's porch each night to wait for her to come home from work, to plead with her to change her mind. Eventually she did.

In essence, that fact summarized Richard Nixon for me then and now.

Here he was, a poor boy from Yorba Linda, which ain't much, believe me. He had no money, no especially great looks, no family background, a father who was barely there, a mother who had to work raising other people's children, and a personality barely covering up a bottomless well of hypersensitivity to everything that happened to him.

So here he was, this nothing from nowhere, and look where he had gotten by sheer persistence and will-power. Kennedy had all that charisma and all that money. Lyndon Johnson had great big steel balls that clanked when he walked across the room. Eisenhower was made of leather inside and out. But Nixon was, to me, always the outsider trying desperately to cover up his fear and his loneliness and act as if he were one of the boys.

Even as a child, I could see that Nixon, alone among politicians, actually bled when he was attacked. Look at him talking about Checkers. Look at him on the night he lost to Kennedy. Listen to him telling the press in Los Angeles in 1962 that they wouldn't have Richard Nixon to kick around anymore. This was not a Ronald Reagan, tough from the inside out, and not a Jimmy Carter, wrapped in a trance of religiosity. This was a man who bled, a real live human being with feelings.

In fact, to compound my felonies, I have always believed that the main reason the press and many, many other Americans hated Richard Nixon had nothing to do with his politics. (William Buckley is far more conservative than Nixon, and he is invited to the best dinner parties in Manhattan.) No, the reason the press liked to go after Richard Nixon, why it became a national sport to go after Richard Nixon, was the same as the reason children in a school yard pick certain children to taunt and certain ones to ignore: Human beings like to go after other human beings who will show their hurt.

I do not pretend that mine is an original theory. Far from it. The part that's *my* feeling about Richard Nixon is that he was always, all his life, that child taunted in the school yard. He tried—oh, how he tried—to pretend that he had a rhinoceros skin. He tried to pretend that he was tough and that "the hotter it gets, the cooler I get."

It didn't fool me. I could see in any press conference, in any give-and-take with reporters, that Richard Nixon was bleeding profusely, that his opponents could smell it, and that they wanted more.

I have to say that after 60 years of this kind of struggle, Richard Nixon had probably even fooled himself about who he was. He might even have believed that he was the big, tough, conservative gunfighter that all the liberals were after. But to me, the siege of Richard Nixon in the Watergate years had nothing to do with conservatives and liberals. It had everything to do with bullies and school yards and victims. I had been the playground victim enough to know which side I was on.

In 1971, when I was working at the Federal Trade Commission behind fiberboard walls, I stopped reading the replies of the dog-food companies about their advertising and strolled across Pennsylvania Avenue to the National Archives and walked into its cool, marble reception room, with the brass engravings of the Founders and their words. The thought suddenly struck me that movies and TV shows were a sort of national archive as well. They told of how the nation felt at any given moment and what the nation was willing to believe.

In a day I wrote an article about how the movies of 1971 predicted with perfect clarity that despite all the qualms about Richard Nixon's policies, the public wanted a Machiavellian, cunning, *seemingly* dominant type as President, almost a Godfather figure. That meant RN. By a small miracle, the article appeared almost instantly in *The Wall Street Journal.* Within one day after the appearance of the article, my immensely fat secretary, an Okie who actually brought her children to work and let them play in the corridor outside my office, buzzed me to say that there was a "Mister Hollerman" on the line. I picked up the phone and heard a pleasant woman voice say, "Mr. Haldeman will be with you in one moment." *Click-click,* and then a voice like a buzz saw in low gear said, "Ben, let's get together and talk about your article."

That day at lunch, instead of eating in the FTC cafeteria (whose special that day was fried turbot, $1.15, with green beans, tea, and a roll), I ate at the White House with H. R. "Bob" Haldeman. In a basement room called the "White House Mess," I sat across from "Bob" at a small table. "Bob" told me that he had been impressed with my article.

He had also been able to show it to "The President," and "The President" agreed there was something there. Haldeman looked at me with his steel-gray eyes; his crew cut, which gave him the air of a religious fanatic; and his high forehead, reminding me of a bank vault. "Ben," he said in a perfectly sincere way, "how would you like to come over here to work at the White House?"

"Doing what?" I asked.

"Writing a comprehensive study of how the mass media reflects our political and social views or doesn't reflect them," he said. "That would help us shape our own TV commercials for the 1972 campaign."

"You mean the President has decided to seek a second term?" I asked. Haldeman laughed, and I laughed, too, and I took the job. It would be fun working with a jolly steel buzz saw, far from the winos and the cardboard walls, right there in the White House, helping the child in the school yard who was now President. It would be a big, big step above working on dog-food commercials with a secretary who brought her children to work.

It had nothing to do with politics. It was about a chance to get out of a pit, to work on something big, somewhere important, for someone whose personality had always touched me.

Her Only Sin
1985

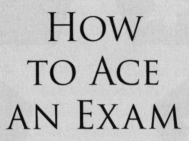

HOW
TO ACE
AN EXAM

IT IS THAT TIME OF YEAR when Tommy is taking exams in school. Like any other sane person, he doesn't like this time of year. So, to lighten his load, I sent him the following bulletin. Take it to heart, all students and parents:

For any exam in history, here is the answer: All human history is the struggle between systems that attempt to shackle the human personality in the name of some intangible good on the one hand, and systems that enable and expand the scope of human personality in the pursuit of extremely tangible aims. The American system is the most successful in the world because it harmonizes best with the aims and longings of human personality while allowing the best protection to other personalities.

For your exam in religion: All religions attempt to meet and answer man's most basic fears and aspirations and reassure man in his wishes to accommodate himself to a very difficult life and a certain death. The religions that do this best are those that offer the most hopeful vision, that which harmonizes best with human personality.

For your exam in art or literature: All great art and literature, all lasting art and literature, attempt to express something lasting and permanent about the human condition and to explain its pains and contradictions and joys through the depiction of the specific and the concrete. Art or literature or music that fails to do this does not last.

I believe he cannot fail to get all A's now, but then maybe in today's world he also has to add some notes about Amerikan Imperialism and the repression implicit in the Bush Doctrine.

The American Spectator Online
12/15/2004

In Hollywood, It's All a Question of Servants and Masters—or Servants and Mistresses

HERE I AM at Morton's on Monday. Twenty-four hours ago, *tout* Hollywood was here at the post-Oscars party. I was not invited. The party was not given by the people who run Morton's. No, the party was given by the people who run *Vanity Fair,* and, again, I was not invited. The party was also given by a fabulously rich producer named Steve Tisch, and, again, I was not invited.

Remember those parties in high school where only the coolest kids were invited? Well, it's sort of like that. I was simply not cool enough to be invited, and I guess that's pretty much that.

However, I am here tonight, when you don't need an invitation. I'm with my pal and producer of my show Al Burton. We're joined by the lovely P., a woman who was a guest on my show yesterday. (Yes, we work on Sundays.) She had such a great Louise Brooks hairdo and was so young and lovely that all of us on the show fell madly in love with her. She has an interesting work history, too.

She breezes in the door in superhigh heels, holding a cigarette in a holder but without her Louise Brooks 'do. She does have on her ladder-textured stockings and still looks pretty good, but not like yesterday.

"I was the Shiseido girl and the Stella Artois girl, and lots of other girls, too," she says. "I could make $10,000, even $12,000, in a day. But I was on the freeway thinking about how short a model's career is, and I had an epiphany."

"Yes?" Al and I ask.

"Life is short but death is long," she says.

"Brilliant," I respond.

"So, as soon as I got home, I went online to find out where I could study to be a funeral director. And within a few days, I had my scalpel and my needles and my microscope and I was studying 'cases,' which is what we call bodies, to get them ready for embalming."

"You are kidding," I say. "I hope you're kidding."

"Not at all," she says. "No one but a few people have any idea of how much funeral directors make in salary.

They start at $120,000, and it doubles every year forever."

"That's clearly impossible, because at that rate, you would have all of the wealth of the world in about 20 years."

"Well, it's something like that," she says. "Maybe it doesn't double every year. I have to go step into the parking lot and have a cigarette. Help me pick out a different color for my cigarette holder. I have a choice of five different holders."

I go out with her to the parking lot, where she falls into conversation with a man from Canada who turns out to be an embalmer. He looks the part: slicked-back white hair, large, but a ghostly white. They fall into conversation, and I go back to Al.

In front of us are Kenny and his pals, including the lovely Dotty, who is staring angrily at me. She has a crush on me, even though I'm poor. Then there is a table of Irwin and Susie Russell, who look happy. Then there is Mr. Popeil with his incredibly beautiful wife, who seems to be pregnant again. Wow, does she look great. She's wearing a low-cut dress and, wow, does she look great beyond words.

Pam Morton is there with my wife. They're talking about summer camps. I want our son to go to one. He wants to stay home and play video games.

"You probably think I want to have this girl as my secret girlfriend," I say to Al. "But I have no interest in her except as a guest on my talk show. For me, there is no sex in Hollywood except for when I cuddle my Puppy-Wuppy and rub her ears, and that's not really sex."

"Anything you say," says Al.

"Sex in Hollywood is a strange thing, and besides, I'm married," I tell Al.

He nods quietly. "P. asked us to get her a Sidecar to drink," Al reminds me. "I wonder why she wants that."

"Who cares? I want to write an article about sex in Hollywood. The point of the piece is that there is no sex, as most people know it, in Hollywood.

"As the ordinary working stiff in Iowa knows it, sex is a way of sharing yourself with someone else. At least I think that's what it's supposed to be. Anyway, there's supposed to be some mutuality.

"But in Hollywood, it's all a question of servants and masters, or servants and mistresses. The idea is to get as much work—sex work—as possible out of the girl without doing anything that in any way opens yourself up to her.

"You can pay her with money to keep her away, or you can give her a connection with an agent, or you can invite her to parties where she might find an agent. But you cannot, under any circumstances, have a meeting of the minds or anything remotely close.

"The other is a servant, a technician called in to supply temporary closeness and the pop of sex. But your own person—well, as a Hollywood player, your own person is sacred. It's between you and your Maker, between you and your producer or agent. It's not to be shared over something as trivial as sex.

"All of these women with their breasts and their legs and their great sex techniques are interchangeable with the guy who fixes the pool cleaner or the compressor on the air-conditioning. So are the muscle boys. The inner kernel of the Hollywood player cannot even be approached in a meaningful way with sex. Drugs, yes, but not sex.

"Charlie Sheen showed the heart of Hollywood when he said that the point of having call girls is not that you pay them to come—you pay them to go."

"Depressing," says Al.

"Or maybe that's the way it always is with power players. They're far too into themselves to care much about someone else of any kind at all. Sex might let you into the weaker sisters, but the *shtarkers*—no, they are far too guarded for that kind of entrée to work."

"More depressing," says Al.

"Well, not for us. None of it applies to us, because we're Untouchables, not even worthy of being invited to the Oscars party. We still have feelings for our dogs and our families."

At that point, P. comes back and talks for a long while, but frankly, I don't listen to what she has to say. I have to prepare for my shows tomorrow. Plus, my dog is waiting in the car.

Most of all, I have to realize that since I have a wife of 30 years whose every footstep is precious to me, I'll never be a Hollywood player. It's a good feeling.

Monday Night at Morton's
4/7/1999

Some Things I Don't Know, and One Thing I Do

WE'VE HAD A LOT OF MATERIAL lately in this column ["Everybody's Business," in *The New York Times*] about interest rates and money supply and inflation and oil and other sordid money matters, so now maybe some loftier subjects are in order. Consider this a little letter of investing advice to the fathers of young kids who are maybe divorced or separated from the kids' mom or who may be still married but are far too busy with the daily grind or the playoffs or the boys at the bar to spend a lot of time with their young kids.

Not long ago, on New Year's Eve, in fact, my writing partner and financial advisor, Phil DeMuth, came out to visit me at our home in Rancho Mirage with his wife, Julia, and his five-year-old adorable daughter, Olivia. We had New Year's Eve dinner at our club. Olivia heard me talk about how great the view of the stars is from our backyard. When we got back to our house, she asked if she could go look at the stars. Phil, Olivia, and I went out to the grassy area (actually, a green of a golf course) behind the house. I told her to look up in the sky. "I can't see," she said, although the stars were gleaming like Times Square.

Phil said, "I'll hold you on my shoulders," and lifted her up onto his 6'5" frame.

"Oooh," she said, "now I see all the stars. They're beautiful."

Now, I thought, *from Earth to the nearest of those stars is millions of miles, maybe more. Having been put on her father's shoulders added an incalculably small fraction to Olivia's closeness to the stars. But it made all the difference in the universe that she was standing on her father's shoulders and she was being lifted up by his love for her.*

That's it, I thought. *With our fathers lifting us up, we get encouragement, belief in ourselves, confidence that we can reach out and grab the stars for ourselves. Without our fathers' lifting us up, we are out in the yard in the dark.*

It was an especially poignant moment for me because the night before, I could not sleep. To soothe myself, I counted all of the jobs my father had gotten me, the homework he helped me do, the articles and books he helped me write, the advice he had given me about life and about money. It was a long list, and I fell asleep when I had barely started. I dreamed that my father was back, alive and smiling at me instead of having died in 1999. In my dream, I fell to my knees and begged him to never go away again. He smiled and laughed and then disappeared, and I woke up in a sweat.

Now, there is a lesson here. Lately, I have been thinking of how little I know about finance and economics. I think I know more than most people, but there are some huge subjects I know nothing about. For example, I don't see how we are ever going to slow down the current account deficit, which is currently running at very roughly $1 trillion a year against us. I don't see when the acquisition of U.S. assets by the Chinese, Japanese, and petro states is going to end. My father used to famously say that if a thing cannot go on forever, it will stop. But will it stop with the United States being a colony of the major exporters? Will it stop with the dollar worth one-fourth of what it's now worth? I keep thinking that America started as a colony and maybe we are going to end as a colony. I know that's far-fetched, but I don't see how a nation that behaves like a college student who has just gotten his first credit card is ever going to see international solvency again. There must be an answer, but I just have no idea of what it will be.

Likewise, U.S. average wages adjusted for inflation have not risen in any meaningful way in about 30 years (more or less). Wages here are constrained in manufacturing by Far Eastern competition, and this restraint ripples through the whole economy except where prices can be fixed, such as in the executive suite and at law firms. What will happen in America as wages stop rising and social friction grinds without being lubricated by generally rising prosperity? How will we solve the health-care crisis? The federal government is already tapped out and the medical establishment is bleeding America white. Where will the money come from to fix the health-care crisis?

I also have no clue what the solution to vast inequality between the blacks and other racial groups in America will be. Education would seem to be the answer, but blacks lag whites and Asians of the nation so badly in education that this avenue would not seem to work, at least not immediately. There must be a solution, but what is it?

I also have no idea why Americans hate oil companies so much. Is it a residual resentment from the days of John D. Rockefeller and his monopoly in oil? Is it because some liberals in media and in Congress think there is a cabal of Texas oilmen running the nation the way Oliver Stone showed it in *Nixon?* Do they think Big Oil is not just one player in a vast commodity market worldwide, subject to its whims as much as anyone at a gas station, sometimes making big profits, other times making less than it spends on exploration and development? I love the oil companies for making gasoline, natural gas, and heating oil available to me for far less than the price of premium bottled waters. (For the record, I give speeches as part of my livelihood, and it is likely in the course of events in the next year or two that an oil company will hire me to speak, although this is just an expectation and no one has paid me now or in the past to speak up for the people who let me drive my big American car, wife, and dogs to Rancho Mirage from West Hollywood for less than the price of a good meal at McDonald's.) Maybe the hatred of the oil companies is just because we are so totally dependent on them, and that makes us resent them the way teenagers resent their parents for the same reason. (How well I know.)

So, as I say, there is a lot I do not know. But I know that investment in your children is usually a pretty damned good investment. I do know it pays off big (although you don't know it when they're teenagers, I assure you). I know that investment in your parents pays off all of the time. Phil is the smartest investment manager I know. His results with my paltry savings have been very happy for me. But even he cannot predict the market with a little bit of precision. But he can predict that his daughter will remember the night he showed her the stars from the desert.

Or let me put it another way: None of us can predict or read the future. But we can read the past, and we can learn from it. That glowing moment on the 14th green under the stars, New Year's Eve 2005, all of the gilded memories of parents and children, of those we loved when we still had them with us . . . they'll all be gone and we'll be alone and wishing we had done more with them. Or we actually can enjoy them more now, while we still can.

The New York Times
1/15/2006

WHY BOTHER TO HAVE SUCH THOUGHTS AT MORTON'S? IT'S ALMOST TREASON

A WOMAN LAWYER, whom I will call "A.," walks over to our table with her friend, a mighty producer whom I will call "M." They sit down with us at our mighty booth.

"Have you seen *Saving Private Ryan?*" asks A.

"No, I have not," I say. "I would like to, but I've been busy."

"It's a great story, wonderfully told," says A. "Magnificent. And you know that Spielberg has a back end on that thing that you wouldn't believe. But he's sharing it 50-50 with Tom Hanks, who is his best friend, and they're just making money like you wouldn't believe."

"You have to admire Spielberg," says M. "He's making movies about things that matter. Things that count. Not just what happens to be on his mind as what's hip in Hollywood that day.

"And he wasn't attached when Paramount first started developing it. He attached himself and DreamWorks because he loved the material. He's that kind of guy. Yes, he makes money, but he also makes things that count and that tell young Americans about life and what matters."

"Those first few minutes when the troops are landing at D-day and all those guys are getting killed," says A. "They're amazing. He deserves a lot of money for showing that."

"I wonder how much money the guys who landed at Normandy got paid for that day's work?" I ask, but everyone scowls at me, so I hide my head in shame.

Still, I'm sure it's a great movie, but I'm also sure there are a lot of guys in VA hospitals and nursing homes who fought at Normandy who never even have a visitor. And will die broke.

Well, why bother to have such thoughts at Morton's? It's almost treason.

Monday Night at Morton's
9/9/1998

SOMEONE IS PUTTING ETHER INTO THEIR GLASSES ...

I HUSTLED OVER HERE TODAY after a long, long day on the set of a second sequel to *Casper*. This one is called *Casper III: A Magical Friendship*. I play a man variously called "Milquetoast Man" and "Nerdy Dancing Instructor" in two scenes. In one, a very fat ghost spills food on me and drools on me. In the other scene, I ask Cathy Moriarty to dance. She says, "Scram, loser!" and I slink away.

We didn't finish until after 8 P.M., so I am late for Morton's. S., a lovely, ambitious woman with whom I work in promoting my show, *Win Ben Stein's Money*, sits with me at a different table from the usual. This one is not next to the door but on the other side of the room under an immense mirror. Next to us is the Marvin Davis ensemble: Marv; his lovely wife, Barbara; the lovely Jackie Collins; Sidney Poitier; and some other people I don't know. They are laughing like mad insanity, apparently at some kind of recurring joke.

The joke is that whenever one of them mentions a movie studio or a network or a car company, someone else says, "Have you bought that yet, Marvin?" and then everyone laughs with a rich, deep, almost scary cackle. The laughter is so deep, it shakes the table.

Behind Marvin is another billionaire, Sumner Redstone, controlling boss of Viacom, which includes Paramount, Simon & Schuster, and many other entities. He looks cheery. He's with Len Goldberg, a famous producer and studio head, and his wife, Wendy. They all look amazingly happy.

In fact, the people on my new side of the restaurant look much happier than they usually look nearer to the door. Is it the new year? Is it sitting near the mirror? What is it?

Sitting at one of the banquettes is my old pal Hal Gaba, who has seemingly grown rich in a variety of businesses. He's in shirtsleeves, and so are three other men at his table. One of them looks familiar. He stops Sumner Redstone to talk as Sumner walks by. I hear the word *stations*. Makes sense, because the man in shirtsleeves is John Muse, yet another billionaire, this time from a series of investments in radio stations, among other sources.

"How come you guys, alone among the diners here, are in shirtsleeves?" I ask Hal Gaba.

"Because we are so rich, we don't care what other people think," Hal says cheerfully.

I done tol' you and tol' you that the people on my new side of the room look unusually happy.

Beautiful but wacky Dotty sits with Kenny and his radio millions and the aging Rat Pack and looks extremely agitated. Once in a while she glares at me, for reasons I know not. But she is on the unhappy side of the room.

I was and am on the happy side.

S. talks to me for hours about her coup in putting radio-station stickers on pizza cartons and on the edges of displays at record stores.

If I hear any more about radio-station stickers, I'm going to take off my clothes and start singing 'America the Beautiful.'"

"Hey," I say. "Let's play *Win Ben Stein's Money*. What is the largest country in area in the world?"

"Africa," she says cheerfully.

"No, a country," I say. "Not a continent, a country."

"Africa," she says again.

"No, not Africa. Africa is a continent. I was asking about countries."

"Oh, yeah," she says. "Kenya?"

Now, where that came from I have no idea. I tell her the answer—Russia—and then I ask, "What is the second-largest country in area in the world?"

Unhesitatingly, S. answers, "Africa."

Okay, I think. *Another avenue of conversation is in order.* "What is the most populous country in the world?"

Without a second's delay, she says, "Africa."

"You obviously have Africa on your mind," I say. "I wonder why."

"Well, because I went to see Victoria Falls over the Zambezi River and white-water rafted down the Zambezi, and those are listed as two of the seven natural wonders of the world."

"Listed by whom? I'm not familiar with that list."

"Well, by everybody," says S.

I'm beginning to figure out why everyone on this side of the room is so happy. Someone is putting ether into their glasses. Or maybe it's chloral hydrate. But the people on this side of the universe of Morton's are flying. Radio flying. Good night.

Monday Night at Morton's
4/1/1998

WALK SHILOH'S BATTLEFIELDS, LEAVE WITH LESSONS FOR TODAY

I HAVE NEVER SEEN a more beautiful spot than the battlefield at Shiloh, Tennessee, where in the first week of April 1862, the bloodiest battle ever fought until that time in North America took place.

The monuments appear out of nowhere and startle the visitor with their bulk and simplicity. The sky goes on forever, and birds sing and cavort where cannons and minié balls killed thousands 139 years ago.

Here the Union forces made a base camp on the banks of the Tennessee River and waited for reinforcements. On April 6, the Rebels attacked at just before dawn. The Confederates at first had the upper hand. But the starving Southerners paused to eat the Unionists' breakfast, then were stopped cold for several hours by desperate resistance at a sunken road. Eventually, the Rebels drove back the defenders and captured hundreds, maybe thousands. However, the Unionists got their reinforcements overnight and pushed back the Southerners.

More than 1,700 Confederates, mostly brand-new to combat, died during those two days, as did about the same number of Unionists. Most of the Union troops are buried in a gloriously beautiful cemetery overlooking the Tennessee River. The dead Confederates are mostly buried in mass graves on the southwestern portion of the battlefield.

By great prudence and foresight, this sacred soil is spectacularly preserved as the Shiloh National Military Park. But all over the Southeast, important battlefields are getting wiped off the map for subdivisions and strip malls. From Brice's Crossroads in Mississippi, where "that Devil," Nathan Bedford Forrest, tore up a larger Northern force; to the stunning hunt country of Virginia near Upperville; to Manassas, where Bull Run I and II were fought; to The Wilderness in east central Virginia, places where the key battles of the Civil War were fought are either in jeopardy or going fast under the bulldozer's pitiless blade.

This is criminal. There is no more important preservation in America than saving this land consecrated, as Lincoln said, by American blood. Groups such as the

Civil War Preservation Trust do their best, but a concerted federal program is needed today, not tomorrow.

I had another thought at that battlefield: *Why aren't more people here?* It was a perfect midsummer day. Including at the spartan visitors' center, I saw maybe 30 people, maybe fewer. At Disneyland, where fictitious animals are big attractions, 30,000 come in a day. At sporting events that are forgotten in a week, 50,000 come. When cruel contests are held on TV to determine who can absorb the most humiliation while chasing money and 15 minutes of fame, tens of millions watch.

Here, where great issues were decided by the sacrifice of Americans, where the natural landscape is perfection, there is almost no one. Something is very wrong with our national value system.

My thoughts also went to the tragedy of the Civil War, which came about in part because of the intense sectional discord over slavery, an unspeakable horror. The disgrace is that the intemperance of both sides led to terrible rancor and bloodshed.

Now the nation also faces grave divisions over abortion, racial contentiousness, and other issues, although none nearly as severe as slavery. It is the task of the nation's leaders to resolve these issues in a way that bloodshed within this country is never even contemplated. We are fortunate to have a President whose stock-in-trade is his good nature and his willingness to see both sides of every issue. You may mock him for his syntax, but few can match his goodwill or readiness to compromise. Had there been many like him in the high ranks of the North and South in the 1850s and 1860s, perhaps we would have never heard of Shiloh.

Of all my thoughts, however, the uppermost was of the individual boys who here died in anguish, their blood and life ebbing as they lay in pain and thirst and heat and terror. This happened because their leaders lacked the foresight or compassion to be able to avoid war. Now they are part of the history of failed policies—a lesson for us all, if only we choose to visit it.

USA Today
8/8/2001

THE REAL LINES IN LIFE ARE BETWEEN THE BIG SCAMMERS AND THE SMALL

IT'S A LANGUID NIGHT here at Morton's. We're having a super heat wave. The high today was over 90 degrees in West Hollywood. It's still hot out in the parking lot, where the Mercedes and Beemers lurk next to my lowly Acura.

Barron and Steve are here with me, trying to talk me into buying a private jet. A Citation is what it's called. "How much will that set me back?"

"About 700 thou," says Barron cheerfully.

"That's too much. How much will it be to run the damned thing every year?"

"About 250," Barron says, even more cheerfully.

"That's way, way, way too much."

"But think of how much better you'll feel whenever you travel," Barron says with evident sincerity.

"If I feel that much better for a few years, I'll be broke," I said. "I don't think it feels that great to be broke."

Steve looked at me earnestly. "It doesn't feel good at all. Take it from me. Not good at all."

Across the room, Ron Perelman ate quietly with some pals. He beamed and waved to me. I wonder if, in some older regime, when the nobility came out of their castles and saw a character actor and ink-stained wretch, they waved at him.

Behind us, Dennis Holt sits. He just sent me a really nice set of timepieces for my son—a little airplane clock, a little clock like a porpoise, another clock. What a friendly, kind guy.

Across the hall, lo and behold, and farther down into the room, out of sight of the curious, is Mickey Rourke. Talk about a talented guy. . . .

Then there are two beautiful girls at the bar, sitting with their backs to the famous artist Julian Schnabel, who is examining a painting with Peter Morton, who owns the painting in question. As the girls turned to troll the bar area, I notice that one of them is Kekili, the most beautiful girl on Earth, even more beautiful than Kath, the world's most beautiful call girl. Kekili is a Hawaiian jewel of about 22. I met her when she was waiting tables at a restaurant on Sunset Plaza. She's a fledgling actor, natch.

She has already been in many calendars and a swimsuit edition of *Playboy,* although with her swimsuit on for a major change.

She is a combination of Polynesian and Filipino, and pure gorgeous. She worked for me as a messenger for a few months, but she was far too unreliable to keep on the payroll. Now, here she is with a pretty *haole* girl, and she wants to talk to us. All heads swivel toward our table as she strolls over.

"We have a problem," she says. "It's about money."

What a shock!

"This is my roommate, Nancy. Her bank says she put a large forged check in her account, then wrote checks against it and used up all the money before the bank figured out the check was forged. But she didn't do it."

The roommate looked demurely offended. "I have no idea how that $10,000 check even got into my account," she said.

"Well, if you didn't do it, there should be no problem," I said. "After all, you just show them that the endorsement on the big check wasn't your signature and the endorsements on the checks that emptied the account weren't yours either, and you're all set."

"That's just the problem," Kekili said. "The endorsements were obviously forged by someone who really knows what he's doing, because they look just like Nancy's signature. The bank is already telling her they're calling the FBI."

"I see."

Steve is a former detective in Fort Worth. He actually laughed. Kekili probably did not quite get the laugh. "I know," she said. "It's really evil."

"It is," I agreed.

"We wondered if you would be her lawyer," Kekili said, nodding at Nancy.

"I don't think so. I've never practiced in California. I'm only a member of the Connecticut bar."

"What about your wife?" Kekili asked.

"She doesn't do criminal work," I said.

Kekili and Nancy wandered off. How sad for them. They are in a room where the smallest scams are a thousand times bigger than what Nancy tried.

They have no clue at all about where they are. They're like finger painters trying to get something hung on the wall at the National Gallery of Art. Well, I guess we all have to start somewhere.

Speaking of which, in walked my wife with Pam Morton, sister of the owner. Luckily, Kekili had already left.

After I talked to my wife and Pam for a moment, I schmoozed with Irwin Miller of Disney about how independent boards of directors should be. Then I walked to the men's room. On the way, I saw Patti, a young woman who used to hang out at the bar all the time long ago, then hooked up with a con man who fleeced her out of her tiny life savings.

"I can't believe what happened," she said in a flat voice. "I just bought a new car. And now it's been stolen. Right from my garage."

Steve was right behind me. "You sure it wasn't repossessed?"

Patti laughed. "What's the difference?" she asked.

I think I've hit on something: The real lines in life here are between the big scammers and the small. Or maybe that's one of the lines.

Social distinctions do matter. The big scammers never have to pay it back.

Outside, the air was dry, clear—perfect.

Monday Night at Morton's
4/9/1997

Stardom? Courage? I Saw Both in the Hollow Eyes of a Small Child

THIS STORY has nothing to do with Hollywood.

A few days ago, while I was in New Hampshire at the Hanover Inn visiting our son at the Cardigan Mountain School, I watched some of a tribute to my former *Honeymoon in Vegas* costar Nicolas Cage.

The part I saw included the staggeringly lovely Elisabeth Shue talking about Cage. "He's so brave," she said. "His artistic choices are just so brave; I think he must be the bravest person I know."

I'm paraphrasing here, and I'm sure Ms. Shue was just excited because she was on camera. But when I think of the word *brave* and also the word *star,* which are suggested by Shue and Cage, I think of a little boy very far from Hollywood.

He is far and away the bravest human being I know right now.

I think I will tell you about him so you know what a real star is like—and don't get fooled by us cheesy Hollywood imitations.

In November of 2000, I was in Little Rock, Arkansas, visiting my in-laws. By total chance, I got an e-mail from a woman in Little Rock who didn't know I was there. She wrote that her nephew had serious tumors in his head. He was about seven and had been through chemo, radiation, and recently, a bone-marrow transplant. She said the boy, whom I will call D., was an immense fan of mine and especially of *Win Ben Stein's Money.* "He doesn't know any of the answers, of course," said the letter, "but he just loves your voice."

I e-mailed back that I was in town, and soon I was in the Arkansas Children's Hospital. D. was in a spacious room in the children's cancer ward, a place of sufficient horror for many lifetimes but a place where the nurses and doctors were clearly working overtime to save lives and to keep up a cheery attitude.

There were stuffed animals and toys everywhere. I brought the tyke a little train set and some other toys I don't recall. He was in a sterile room with two sets of doors to keep out infection, because his chemo had virtually wiped out his white blood cells.

His mother was lying on the bed with him. He had about a dozen tubes going into his chest all at one central point. His hair was gone, his eyes were sunken, but still he giggled when I entered the room.

"It's Ben Stein," his mother kept saying. His father, who had brought me over, added, "He's not on TV; he's right here."

"You see all those tubes going into him?" his mother asked. "He calls those his Ben Stein lines, and when they hurt, he says it's Ben Stein who's taking the pain, not him."

I said I doubted I could take that much pain. The child just looked at me, and then he played with his train while looking at me.

After I left, I made an arrangement to help the family in a way that is easy for a TV star (even a lowly cable one) and hard for an Army sergeant, which is what the boy's father is. I came back twice more to see D., but he was not doing well, so he could only wave weakly to me from his glassed-in room.

Time passed. I stayed in close touch with D.'s parents. They made a Website for the boy and his many supporters. He had every kind of treatment. He had his ups and his downs. He was free of tumors for a time, and then they came back and he was in and out of the hospital.

Yesterday morning, I got an e-mail from his mother: "D. has had a stroke. His tumors are back, and they are growing. The doctors say it is only a matter of days until he passes. I will keep you informed."

Let me tell you that D. never once complained. He never asked why he had to spend his childhood with tubes in him and in agony from chemo. He never asked why he had to be inside behind glass when other seven-year-olds were outside making snowmen.

His parents barely complained as well. They stuck with him every second and only wanted to serve him and their country.

D. may make a miraculous recovery, or he may enter immortality soon and lay down his poor, cancer-riddled body. I imagine him playing in the next life and making up for the time he has missed, maybe for all eternity. But who knows?

What I do know is that life for most of us is pretty easy. We sometimes go to auditions and don't get parts. I was at one two days ago, where I tried out to be Ralph Fiennes' political advisor in a movie in which he's Prince Charming to J.Lo's Cinderella.

A roomful of beautiful actresses was trying out for smaller roles, some of them complaining mightily about how going to auditions is the worst thing in the world.

And then there's Elisabeth Shue, telling us that making the right acting choices is the bravest thing in the world. And then there are people on TV saying that dieting is the hardest thing in the world.

This is America, and we all have our opinions. But for me, I saw real stardom and courage in the hollow eyes of a little boy in a room at the Arkansas Children's Hospital. I saw real acting genius in his mom and dad and in the nurses keeping up their happy facades while small children lay mortally sick all around them.

There will be no star for D. on the Hollywood Walk of Fame. There will be no table where he is remembered at Morton's—except mine. But he is a true star, shining eternally in a dark night, and he has brought light to everyone he has touched.

Addendum: I wrote this column on Friday. D.—whose real name is Dillon Rolins—died peacefully on Tuesday night, in Arkansas in the bosom of his family. May God bless his soul. He was an angel, and now he is with the other angels, where he belongs. Nothing I will ever be able to tell you about Hollywood will ever touch the magnificence of this child's courage and innocence. No movie or TV show—however well written, acted, or lit—will ever touch the greatness of his family's devotion. But as you already guessed, this story has nothing to do with Hollywood.

Monday Night at Morton's
3/14/2002

COL. DENMAN'S LUGER

A FEW DAYS AGO, a package arrived in the mail from the widow of my late father-in-law, Colonel Dale Denman, Jr., of Heber Springs, Arkansas. I opened it and there was a leather holster, and inside it, a German Luger pistol. My father-in-law had taken it from a captured German officer in early 1945 and kept it for almost 60 years. He had left his wife instructions that I was to get it.

You've probably seen ones like it in movies. They look deadly. The Germans made a lot of them to give as a standard sidearm to officers in World War II. I wonder what this pistol did. Kill totally innocent Jews? Lead a charge against British or American soldiers? I just know that after a fierce firefight near the Czech border, it was captured, along with its keeper, by my father-in-law.

Now, I have it next to my bed in a drawer along with many letters from Col. Denman.

I know there are a lot of these Lugers around. You can buy them at antique-gun shops and gun shows. But this one is special to me. Here is what it says:

My brave father-in-law, representative of tens of millions of American men and women who have gone off to fight for freedom, fought against cruel, tenacious enemies. They often lost their lives in so doing. They prevailed, and I get to live in spectacular freedom—glorious, bright freedom—every day because men like Col. Denman were as brave as they were.

I have relatives and friends who get out of bed every morning and do an hour of exercise to keep them fit. I don't do that. My exercise is that I get out of bed and hit my knees and thank God for waking up in America, where I live in peace and freedom . . . no Gestapo chasing me, no KGB putting me in the Gulag, no Hamas blowing me up. All thanks to men like Col. Denman and the heroism he showed capturing this Luger.

That exercise does not keep me thin, most assuredly. But it does set me up for my day by putting me into an attitude of gratitude for the men and women who wore the uniform and still wear the uniform in Iraq and Afghanistan and everywhere. My wife is not giving me

any presents this holiday season, and I am only giving her one. Instead, we are sending gifts to the American fighting men and women in Iraq and Afghanistan to show we're thinking of them. This Luger reminds me it's the least we can do.

The American Spectator Online
12/10/2004

ISN'T IT GREAT TO BE THIN?

I'M HERE WITH SOME PALS from the world of commercials: Marcia Hurwitz, my powerful, lovely, thin agent; and L.A.'s new sensation of the radio airwaves, April Winchell, who is doing some hilarious bank spots blasting Wells Fargo.

Mary Margaret, world's strongest woman and now my nutritionist, is also joining us. Her job is to yell at me and tell me how disgusting fatty foods are and how disgusting I am to eat them. I have lost a bit of weight on this regime. Fun, huh?

Right next to us, Kath, the world's most beautiful call girl, is dining with someone I vaguely recognize from the world of low finance. She looks as if she is about to blow up into a hundred pieces, and then each of them will turn into a cluster bomb and wipe out Morton's. I'm not sure I have ever seen anyone look quite as tense.

At the door, Steve Tisch comes strolling in. He has gained back the weight he lost for the Oscars—or at least some of it. Losing weight is not easy, take it from me.

Steve, son of one of the world's richest men and nephew of another, is in today's *Wall Street Journal,* telling how he likes the simple life, which is described as *la vie* of a ranch in Montana, a private jet, your own chef, and a custom-made log home with a screening room. This sounds simple indeed—if your uncle owned CBS and you produced *Forrest Gump.*

Steve sat on the left. In front of him were Jon Dolgen and Jeff Katzenberg. I got up to talk to them. Just as I did, Ron Perelman, owner of Revlon, among many other nice things, walked over in his trademark white cotton shirt without a tie. With him was his lieutenant, Donald Drapkin. Both carried unlit cigars. This makes sense, since Perelman also owns one of the biggest cigar companies in the world, if not the biggest.

"You look thin, Ben," Jeff said. "Have you been dieting?"

"You bet," I said cheerily.

Jon looked at me searchingly. "You do look thin," he said. "Are you all right?"

See, this is the problem in L.A. You want to be thin, to be sure. But you don't want to be so thin that you give the impression you might have AIDS.

I am still about, oh, 50 pounds from that level, but I am not going to quit until I get to where people think I'm sick.

"Did you get your expense account cut?" I asked Jeff. "I hardly see you out any longer."

"Geffen won't let me eat out," he said, and slapped me on the shoulder. "I have to pack my lunch."

Back at my table, we were discussing whether I should have a one-man show at a comedy club. Frankly, I don't think so.

Gary Lieberthal came by with his two incredibly cute kids. The daughter asked for my autograph. Then she went running outside and told a white-haired man getting out of a limo that she had just gotten my autograph. "I just got Ben Stein's autograph," she said. (I know because her dad came back and told me.)

The white-haired man was Mr. Lew Wasserman. He showed absolutely no sign of recognition and cruised inside to join a large party near us.

That man was a god when I first came here. Now he's another old rich person. This is a lot better than being an old poor person, to be sure, but you get the picture. *Sic transit gloria mundi.*

Kath's date got up suddenly and walked out to the parking lot. I went over to talk to her. She looked as if her jaw had been wired shut.

"I'm having a panic attack," she said.

"Why?"

"I don't know. I just know that I feel as if I was going to just get up and start screaming. Screaming that I hate all of these rich pigs and their wives with their big diamonds."

"Kath, that's not nice."

"But I'm going crazy!" she said. "I'm in a restaurant, and I feel like I'm starving. I feel like all these rich people have taken all the food off the table, and there's none left for me. I feel as if all of the air in the room is being sucked out by Steve Tisch and Ron Perelman, and they didn't leave any for me."

"Go home," I said. "Go home and go to sleep."

"I don't have a ride. I told the guy I was with that I wouldn't do him, and he left."

"I'll give you a ride," I said. "We're almost done."

Back at my table, Mary Margaret said, "Ben, you're becoming anorexic. You're ridiculously thin. You have to eat more. Have the pear stuffed with berries."

Some days, I try to add up how much wealth is in the room. Let's see: Perelman, maybe $4 billion; Tisch, maybe $300 million; Peter Morton, who was in the back of the room, maybe $500 million; Jeff, maybe $60 or $80 mil, with a goddamned lot more on the way from DreamWorks. Then there were a few Drexel players in the back having dinner with Pam Morton. I am not sure what they have.

There is too much money in this room. It's like too many plants in a hothouse. The air just gets too thick to breathe.

I started to feel slightly nauseated. My mother, God love her, throws up when she's around rich people. Maybe I'm catching it. Besides, what do these rich people talk about? I used to eat with rich people long ago. They talked about what was in the *Enquirer.*

On the way out, Ron looked at me and said, "You look great, Ben."

"Isn't it great to be thin?" Mary Margaret asked. "Doesn't it just make your whole world better?"

"It does," I said, "but I used to love eating, and now I hate it. I'm not sure if I'm better off or not."

"Trust me," Mary Margaret said. "If Ron Perelman says you look great, you are a lot better off."

"Why?" I asked, but she did not hear me.

In the car, Kath asked if I thought I would ever leave L.A. Then she cried until I dropped her off in Brentwood, and I went home to my dog.

Monday Night at Morton's
11/5/1996

MOTHER'S DAY

THE MOST PERMANENT feature of life when you are a child is your mother. She is always there telling you to study more, to stand straighter, to clean up your room, to speak more clearly. She is always warning you, cautioning you, telling you what a bleak future you are going to have if you don't mend your ways.

That, at least, was my mother. She had grown up with a father who died when she was nine, had to make it through the Great Depression by studying super hard and getting scholarships, and that was the way she saw life.

And, truth to tell, I didn't like her much for it. I didn't like her paying so much attention to me. I wanted her to leave me alone.

Time passed. My mother didn't leave me alone.

When I went off to college in a city where I knew hardly a soul, a city called New York, my mother wrote me a letter, sometimes two, every day so I would have something in my mailbox at Columbia. There were no e-mails then and long distance was expensive, so she sat down with a pen and paper and wrote me letters, often hilarious, about her life in Maryland.

I had a girlfriend at the University of Chicago one year, and my mother insisted on sending me a plane ticket to go see her—again, so I would not be lonely.

When I went to law school in New Haven, my mother also wrote me every day. She did not want me to be alone or lonely. She had been a lonely child, and she knew it hurt.

When I got married, she called my wife or me every few days and wrote us frequent letters.

When I lost my job at the White House because my boss, Mr. Nixon, resigned, my mother called her high-powered friends until she got me not just one, but many job offers. I didn't take any of them, but there she was, not leaving me alone, again.

She loved dogs and she loved to travel. She was in France when my beloved Weimaraner, Mary, died. She offered to come home to help bury Mary. To Los Angeles.

When she grew old, I would go once a month to visit her and my pop in Washington. When I would leave, she would follow me down the hallway at the Watergate and look at me as if she were trying to work me into her immortal soul forever. Wherever I went, she would be on the phone calling me before anyone else. She would not let me alone.

My mother died unexpectedly of heart failure on April 21, 1997. She left me alone, and I hate it. I hate that there are no more letters from her, no more long last looks while walking down the hall at the Watergate. I still look to see if there are any messages from her at the hotels where I spend most of my time. I have a great wife and she pays attention to me, and I am old by now anyway. But I miss having someone telling me what to do, paying attention to me every single second at every moment of my life. When you are a child, it's a pain and a burden. But love it anyway. The time will come when your mother does leave you alone, and the silence is deafening. And, yes, it's lonely.

CBS News Sunday Morning
5/8/2005

How to Ruin American Enterprise

WE'RE WELL ON OUR WAY to squelching what gives this country an edge. What would it take to kill innovation altogether? As a casual observer of what makes this country work and what stops it cold, I hereby offer a few suggestions on how we can ruin American competitiveness and innovation in the course of this century. I think the reader will agree with me that we are already far down the road on many of them:

1. Allow schools to fall into useless decay. Do not teach civics or history except to describe America as a hopelessly fascistic, reactionary pit. Do not expect students to know the basics of mathematics, chemistry, and physics. Working closely with the teachers' unions, make sure that you dumb down standards so that children who make the most minimal effort still get by with flying colors. Destroy the knowledge base on which all of mankind's scientific progress has been built by guaranteeing that such learning is confined to only a few, and spread ignorance and complacency among the many. Watch America lose its scientific and competitive edge to other nations that make a comprehensive knowledge base a rule of the society.

2. Encourage the making of laws and rules by trial lawyers and sympathetic judges, especially through class actions. Bypass the legislative mechanisms that involve elected representatives and a President. This will stop—or at least greatly slow down—innovation, as corporations and individuals hesitate to explore new ideas for fear of getting punished (or regulated to death) by litigation for any misstep, no matter how slight, in the creation of new products and services. Make sure that lawsuits against drugmakers are especially encouraged so that the companies are afraid to develop new life-saving drugs, lest they be sued for sums that will bankrupt them. Make trial lawyers and judges, not scientists, responsible for the flow of new products and services.

3. Create a culture that blames the other guy for everything and discourages any form of individual self-restraint or self-control. Promote litigation to punish tobacco companies on the theory that they compel innocent people to smoke. Make it second nature for someone who is overweight to blame the restaurant that served him fries. Encourage a legal process that can kill a drug company for any mistakes in self-medication. Make it a general rule that anyone with more money than a plaintiff is responsible for anything harmful that a plaintiff does. Promulgate the pitiful joke that Americans are hereby exempt from any responsibility for their own actions—so long as there are deep pockets around to be rifled.

4. Sneer at hard work and thrift. Encourage the belief that all true wealth comes from skillful manipulation and cunning, or from sudden, brilliant, and lucky strokes that leave the plodding, ordinary worker and saver in the dust. Make sure that society's idols are men and women who got rich from being sexy in public or through gambling or playing tricks, not from hard work or patience. Make the citizenry permanently envious and bewildered about where real success comes from.

5. Hold the managers of corporations to extremely lax standards of conduct and allow them to get off with a slap on the wrist when they betray the trust of shareholders. This will discourage thrift and investment and

ensure that Americans will have far less capital to work with than other societies, while simultaneously developing that contempt for law and social standards that is the hallmark of failing nations. Hold the management of labor unions to no ethical standards.

6. While you're at it, discourage respect for law in every possible way. This will dissolve the glue that holds the nation together and dissuade any long-term thinking. Societies in which the law can be clearly seen to apply to some and not to others are doomed to decay, in terms of innovation and everything else.

7. Encourage a mass culture that spits on intelligence and study and instead elevates drug use, coolness through sex and violence, and contempt for school. As children learn to be stupid instead of smart, the national intelligence base needed for innovation will simply vanish into MTV-land.

Forbes.com
12/23/2002

ELVIS,
R.I.P.

YESTERDAY I DROVE UP TO ARVIN, California, with the girl with the blue-green eyes. Arvin is in the San Joaquin Valley, just east of Bakersfield, in a flat plain that opens suddenly after you reach the Tejon pass in the Tehachapis. The San Joaquin Valley, only an hour and a half from L.A., could not be farther removed from the world of flash, cash, and trash. Arvin, a small farming community, is populated almost exclusively by former Okies who came to California during the Great Depression. None of them got rich, but they made a living and grew to be proud of who they were and what they had endured. The town lies at the end of a row of palm trees in a wide space on Kern County Highway 223.

Most of the buildings in Arvin are low cement structures with flat fronts, painted signs, and one large picture window. The stores and repair shops and the one café are all painted various pastels—pink, blue, brown, orange, yellow. On the sidewalk of the one block of downtown is a list of the churches of Arvin: Southern Baptist, Church of the Nazarene, Pentecostal, Full Gospel, Tabernacle, and the other faiths that were carried in those tin lizzies and Chevies across Route 66, with the dust bowl howling at the back of the mind, and visions of heaven ahead.

I went up there to see what it was like in a town full of old Okies. What did they think about now that a new drought was upon us? What do they think of doctors and lawyers buying all the land as a tax shelter? What do they think? I thought they deserved to have something written about them.

On our way back, across unending fields of cotton, we turned on the radio for the CBS news. At 3 P.M., the announcer came on and played a snatch of "Hound Dog," and I knew, before she said a word, that Elvis Presley was dead. I wondered how the people of Arvin would take it. They probably had a better understanding of him than I ever could. He was more one of them than one of me.

Driving across the eight-lane highway that leads into L.A., through the mountains that were getting covered with fog, I thought about Elvis a lot. I could remember him from elementary school, clear as a bell, singing "Blue Suede Shoes." I could remember him singing "Loving You" in eighth grade, while I danced close with girls for the first time. I could remember him singing "Too Much" and the hard guys and hard girls at the one movie theater in my suburb grooving along with it while I stared out at them from behind the stack of books I carried.

There was his sneer, and there his pompadour, and there his baby fat, and there his pink Cadillac, and there his army uniform, and there his bride and his baby, and there his mansion, and there him in a white jumpsuit at the Las Vegas Hilton. I remembered the crowd in Vegas, screaming when they saw him, screaming with the longing of a lifetime to be part of a man who was salvation in sequins and satin scarves.

And tucked away in my cartons as I moved around the country and back and forth from California were his records, incredibly old-fashioned-looking 45s, with pictures of him in his farm-boy outfit from *Love Me Tender*.

And suddenly he was dead at 42. People told me that Elvis was blowing five grams of coke a day in the last year. I do not know at all. I don't even care that much, except that it probably killed him. He was dead, and all the things I associated with him went floating around and out the funnel of time so that I felt as if 21 years had passed by in an instant of the CBS news.

I was lucky I heard about it on the way back from Arvin, because if I had heard it on Sunset Boulevard, it might not have made me think so much. But driving back from Arvin, while semis and diesels passed me, I had time to think.

And I thought about an 18-year-old Elvis, driving a truck, who becomes a star in a few days . . . and has more money and more money and more money, and women, and houses, and cars, and then drugs . . . and then dies one day, fully clothed, on his bedroom floor, at the age of 42. What if someone had told him that death at 42 on a bedroom floor was what lay ahead? What would he have done? Would he have kept on driving that truck?

I want to know the answer because it tells me something about every kind of wanting to be a star, and a lot of people I know want to be stars, and so do I. What was Elvis telling us?

Last night I bought an Elvis album with his wonderful "I Was the One." I have wanted that song and that album for 20 years, and I got it last night and played that song 20 times, sitting in my living room watching the rain fall on the valley.

This afternoon, as I drove home from the studio, KRTH played Elvis's record of "Old Shep." It's about a boy whose old dog, Shep, is going blind. The vet tells him that the dog is dying and the vet cannot do any more. The boy tries to shoot the dog to put him out of his pain. He wants to kill himself instead. I cried for about two hours when I heard that song.

Later, a friend called me. He's in the record business. Someone had called him from North Carolina and said that he was crippled and losing his sight. He has a daughter who is losing her sight, too. He loves Elvis. His daughter loves Elvis, too. They have every one of his albums. The caller wanted to know how much he could get for them.

I think the people in Arvin could tell him how much those records are worth.

DREEMZ
1978

LET'S STAND FOR SOMETHING

NOW FOR A FEW deathless words about politics.

First, last weekend I spent a bit of time reading a long article in *The New Yorker* about the Democrats' chances in November. The author was a good writer named Jeffrey Goldberg. He, like everyone else, says the Democrats have a real chance to win back the House of Representatives and start subpoenaing everyone at the Bush White House. But, he says, the Democrats have a few problems.

Basically, the core groups of the Democratic Party like abortion and think it's no big deal. Most Americans disagree, and a large number disagree with all of their hearts and souls. Basically, the core groups of the Democratic Party hate the notion of private citizens owning firearms and want strict gun control. A very large number of Americans disagree, and some disagree strongly. The core of the Democratic Party wants to tax the middle class and upper-middle class more and give the money to the teachers' unions. (This last about the teachers' union is my interpretation.) But many Americans like lower taxes.

What Jeffrey Goldberg quotes a number of American Democrat activists as saying at the end of the article is this: Yes, we know what is best to make Americans perfect. Make them like abortion, hate guns, and love taxes. But Americans are imperfect. They like babies, like to be able to protect their homes, and don't like taxes. To win the election, say Goldberg and his sources (I'm summarizing here), the Democrats have to discipline themselves to accept the imperfections of Americans and pretend to go along with them.

I actually started to laugh when I read that part. No wonder Karl Rove can keep pulling out these victories. If the other side really thinks it's an "imperfection" to dislike partial-birth abortion or to want to be able to shoot a rapist or to keep more of the money you make, then Republicans are going to keep on winning elections.

BUT, and this is a huge but, the Republicans have to stand for something. Right now, they are rudderless, drifting, cringing, completely unable to come up with a meaningful statement of what they believe.

It is time for a conference of the party gurus to convene and decide what the party stands for.

I would call it a sort of second Contract with America, only this time not written by the trade association for the big accounting firms.

Here are a few of the points such a declaration might include:

- Unequivocal support for our fighting men, including those accused of misconduct in Iraq up until they are found guilty by an impartial court. Drastic upgrading of military pay. A commitment to treat the families of the military like gold.

- Ironclad opposition to the taking of innocent life by abortion and euthanasia except in the most extreme and rare cases.

- The harshest penalties for those profiteering from the war in any way.

- A clear statement that the party stands with the savers and investors and families of the nation and against the looters and self-dealing, self-serving, wildly overpaid CEOs who steal far more from their stockholders with a fountain pen than Dillinger ever stole with a pistol.

- An energy policy that does not mock and victimize the people who work like demons to bring us energy, namely the oil-company employees; does not punish them for bringing us oil; and at the same time keeps them under constant scrutiny for price-fixing. An energy policy that puts getting to work and doing a job ahead of groundless fears of pollution of beaches and landscapes.

- A retirement-security policy that makes it a national priority to teach Americans of the jeopardy they face unless they get serious about saving in stocks, annuities, bonds, and every other responsible venue for saving.

- A thorough examination of how we treat patients in pain, with a view to a halt to punishing them by denying them the medicines they need to get through their lives without pain or humiliation.

- A serious effort to protect our ports and borders from terrorist threats.

- A complete stop to anything at all that resembles forced busing or the redrawing of school-district lines to compel students to attend one school or another on the basis of race.

- An agonizing reappraisal of whether we should be in Iraq at all.

- A defense policy that truly allows us to defend ourselves against the Islamic threat in fact and not just on paper.

These are just a few ideas. There are, I am sure, many, many others that make sense. But let's stand for something.

The American Spectator
6/7/2006

My Father's Estate

A LETTER FROM AN ILL-MANNERED former high-school classmate of long ago, one of several like it, which I pass on in paraphrase: "I saw that your father had died," she wrote. "He was always so clever about money. Did he leave you a big estate? Did he figure out a way around the estate tax?" It's a rude question, but it has an answer.

My sister and I have been going through my father's estate lately with his lawyer, and we're pawing through old, dusty files to find bank-account numbers and rules for annuities, so maybe it's a good time to think about what my father, Herbert Stein, left to us.

He did indeed leave some money. By the standards we read about in *The Wall Street Journal* or *Sports Illustrated*, it was not worthy of much ink. In any event, because of the class-warfare-based death tax, the amount that will be left is vastly less than what he had saved. As an economist, my father was famous for defending taxes as a necessary evil. But even he was staggered, not long before his death, when he considered the taxes on his savings that would go to the Internal Revenue Service.

The nest egg is going to be taxed at a federal rate of about 55 percent, after an initial exemption and then a transition amount taxed at around 40 percent (and all that after paying estate expenses). When I think about it, I want to cry. My father and mother lived frugally all their lives. They never had a luxury car. They never flew first class unless it was on the expense account. They never in their whole lives went on an expensive vacation. When he last went into the hospital, my father was still wearing an old pair of gray wool slacks with a sewed-up hole in them from where my dog ripped them—15 years ago.

They never had live-in help. My father washed the dishes after my mother made the meatloaf. My father took the bus whenever he could. His only large expenditure in his and my mom's whole lives was to pay for schools for his children and grandchildren. He never bought bottled, imported water; he said whatever came out of the tap was good enough for him. They still used bargain-basement furniture from before the war for their bedroom furniture and their couch. I never once knew them to order the most expensive thing in a restaurant, and they always took the leftovers home.

They made not one penny from stock options or golden parachutes. They made it all by depriving themselves in the name of thrift and prudence and preparing for the needs of posterity. To think that this abstemiousness and this display of virtue will primarily benefit the IRS is really just so galling I can hardly stand it. The only possible reason for it is to satisfy some urge of jealousy by people who were less self-disciplined.

There are a few material, tangible items that an assessor will have to come in to appraise. There are my father's books, from his days at Williams College and the University of Chicago, many of them still neatly underlined and annotated in his handwriting, which did not change from 1931 until days before his death. Most of them are about economics, but some are poetry.

That's another item my father left: his own poetry and his massive prose writings. Very little of it is about anything at all abstruse. There are no formulas and no graphs or charts, except from his very last years. There are many essays about how much he missed my mom when she died, about how much he loved the sights of Washington, about how dismaying it was that there was still so much confusion about basic issues in economics. And there are his satires of haiku about public policy, his takeoffs on Wordsworth and Shakespeare, often composed for a friend's birthday, then sometimes later published.

I suppose there will not be much tax on these because my father was hardly a writer for the large audience. Some of them will go to the Nixon Library, and some will be on bookshelves in the (very small and modest) house my wife and I own in Malibu, a place he found beguiling because he had always wanted to live by the ocean and write. And there's his furniture and his clothes, none of which has any value at all except to me because they remind me of him and because, when I stand near them in his closet, I can still smell his smell of hair and skin and leather shoes, the closet smelling a lot like he smelled when he came home from work in 1954 carrying a newspaper that said there could be no more racial segregation in schools. And there are his mementos of Richard Nixon, his White House cuff links, photos of Camp David, certificates and honorary degrees, and clippings of great events of state. And there are his love letters to and from my mother when they were courting in 1935 and 1936, still tied with light blue ribbon in what was my mother's lingerie drawer, talking about their love triumphing over the dangers of the Depression. I suppose we'll have to place a value on these and have them taxed, too.

But these are the trivia of what he left me and my sister. The really valuable estate cannot be touched by the death tax. The man's legacy to his family has almost nothing to do with anything that can be appraised in dollars and cents.

The example of loyalty and principle: When he had just taken over as the chairman of President Nixon's Council of Economic Advisers, he hired a young staff economist named Ron Hoffman (brother of Dustin Hoffman). Almost immediately, John Dean, then White House counsel, came to see my father to tell him that he had to fire Hoffman. Apparently, Ron Hoffman had signed a public antiwar letter. The FBI, or whoever, said that showed he was not loyal and not qualified. My father said that this was a free country, that Ron Hoffman was hired as an economist not as a political flack for RN, and that he would not be fired because he disagreed with some aspect of Nixon policy. After much worrying, Hoffman was allowed to stay—and performed well.

My father was loyal, and the IRS cannot impound that legacy. When RN ran into every kind of problem after June of 1972, most of which were unearned and a chunk of which was earned, my father never thought of disavowing him or even distancing himself from Nixon. Even though he had an appointment to the University of Virginia in his pocket, Pop several times extended his stay at the White House to help out with the struggles over inflation and recession, and never once publicly said a word against Nixon.

Long after, when Nixon was blasted as an anti-Semite, my father told in print and in person of the Nixon he knew: kind; concerned about all on his staff, regardless of ethnicity; pro-Israel; pro-Jewish in every important cause. My father would never turn his back on a man who had been as conscientious to the cause of peace and as kind to the Stein family as RN had been. *Loyalty.* There is no item for it in the inventory of estate assets to be taxed.

My father lived his life, especially in the latter years of it, in a haze of appreciation. Whatever small faults he could and did find with America, he endlessly reminded anyone who listened that the best achievement of mankind was America—whose current failings were trivial by historical standards—which was in a constant process of amelioration, and which offered its citizens the best chance in history for a good life.

When he did consider the failures of American life in the past, especially institutionalized racism, he did so to note the astonishing progress that had been made in his lifetime. He had no use for those who held up a mirror of faultfinding from the Left or the Right when he could see in his own era what vast improvements in freedom had been made for blacks, Jews, women, Asians, Hispanics, and every other minority.

He appreciated art, especially ballet and opera. He sat for hours in front of the television watching videos of *Romeo and Juliet* or *Les Sylphides* or *Tosca.* He lived to go to the Kennedy Center to see great ballet or opera, and he talked of it endlessly. But he also appreciated art in the form of obscure fountains in front of federal buildings, of the statues of Bolívar and George Washington and

San Martín. He appreciated the intricate moldings on the ceiling of the second floor of the Cosmos Club. He was in awe of the beauty of the mighty Potomac in fall and of the rolling green hunt country around Middleburg and The Plains, Virginia, in summer.

This quality of gratitude for America and for the beauty of life cannot be taxed, at least not so far.

He appreciated his friends and did not differentiate between them on the basis of fame or position. He took the words of his longtime pal Murray Foss at the American Enterprise Institute, a think tank where he hung his hat for many years, into account; and the words of Mrs. Wiggins, who ran the cafeteria at the AEI; and the thoughts of Alan Greenspan or the head of Goldman Sachs; and valued them entirely on their merits to him, not on the basis of how much press or money the speaker had. He never once in my lifetime's recall said that any man or woman deserved special respect for riches—in fact, like Adam Smith, he believed that the pleadings of the rich merited special suspicion. He did not believe that my sister and I should devote our lives to the pursuit of money, and by his life set an example to us of pursuing only what was interesting and challenging, not what paid the most. I never knew him to chase a deal or a job (he never in his whole life applied for a job!) for any other reason except that it was of interest to him. He derived more pleasure from speaking to his pals at the book club of the Cosmos Club about John Keats than he did from giving speeches to trade associations that paid him handsomely.

My father's stance against seeking money for its own sake—so wildly unsuited to today's age, but so reassuring to his children—cannot be taken by the Treasury.

Pop had a way of putting what I thought of as catastrophes into their rightful context. If I was hysterical about losing some scriptwriting job, my father would brush it aside as a basic risk, part of the life I had chosen. If my stocks went down, even dramatically, my father would explain that if I had a roof over my head and enough to eat, I was far, far ahead of the game. Most reassuring, my father would tell me that my family and I could always come to Washington, D.C., and live quietly, keeping him company, for which not a lot of money was required. (My father lived on a fraction of the income from his savings, even allowing for paying for his grandchildren's education.)

Once, about 25 years ago, when my boss treated me unfairly, my father said that if it happened again, I should quit and he would take care of me until I found a job. I never needed to do it, but the offer hung in my mind as a last refuge forever.

This reassurance—that somehow things will be all right, that there is a lot of ruin in a man, as well as in a nation, to paraphrase his idol, Adam Smith—has become part of me, and I can still summon it up when I am terrified because of a huge quarterly tax payment due or a bad day on the market. Again, the IRS taxes it at zero.

My father himself, as far as I know, inherited no money at all from his father. He did inherit a belief that hard work would solve most problems, that spending beyond one's means was a recipe for disaster, that flashy show-off behavior with borrowed money was understandable but foolish. He did inherit enough common sense to tell his son that buying property he would never live in was probably a bad mistake. (He rarely spoke in moral absolutes. He believed instead that humans could and would make individual choices but that there were surely consequences to those choices that could be considered.) He passed these beliefs on to me, although they have become somewhat attenuated by my 20-plus years in the fleshpots of Hollywood. Still, I am one of the only men I know here who has never been drastically short of money (so far), and that I attribute to hearing his rules of prudence.

Most of all, my father believed in loving and appreciating those persons close to him. He stayed close to all his pals from the Nixon days (and would not hear personal criticism of Pat Buchanan, who had been a friend and colleague, although he was bewildered by Pat's stands on many issues). He basked in the pleasure of the company of his colleagues and friends at the American Enterprise Institute, which he thought of as one of his three homes—the Cosmos Club and his extremely modest but well-situated apartment at the Watergate were the others.

He could form attachments readily. Even in his last days in the hospital, he took a liking to a Ukrainian-born doctor and used to refer to him as "Suvorov," after the

Russian general written of glowingly in *War and Peace*—which still sits on the table next to his reading chair, with his notes on little pieces of paper in it.

He grieved like a banshee when my mother died in 1997 and never really got over the loss of a soul mate of 61 years, who literally dreamed the same dreams he did. Once, he wrote my mother a poem (which he called "Route 29") about the beauty of Route 29 north of Charlottesville, Virginia, and the pleasure of riding along it with my mom. He filed it away for further work and never touched it again. The day after my mother's death, he found it—with her reply poem telling of how she hoped to never see those hills and those clouds and those cattle with anyone else but Pop. She had written her poem (which she titled "Only You") and put it back in the file without ever telling him. He survived that terrible loss with the help of a beautiful widow, whom he also came to appreciate and live for. He probably spent more time trying to help her with an annuity problem than he ever did on any financial feature of his own life. A simple call from her inviting him to dinner in her kitchen on Kalorama Circle was enough to make his life complete.

Even in his hospital bed, hearing my son's voice on the phone could make him smile through the fear and the pain. ("He sounds so sweet when he calls me 'Grandpa,'" my father said, beaming even with tubes in him.)

Never once did my sister or I ever ask him for help that he hesitated, let alone declined, to give. Usually this was some research we were too lazy to do, but which he did without any resistance at all. When I was a child and had a chore like leaf raking that I didn't want to do, his simple answer was to say, "Let's do it together. It'll take half as long." I use that with my son almost every day, along with the devotion, and my father's example about his friends from long ago to make my life work. He stayed close with friends from Williams College class of '35, especially Richard Helms of the CIA. He had lunch with one of his pals from Williams, Johnny Davis—class of '33, who had gotten him a job as a dishwasher at Sigma Chi way back when—days before he went into the hospital.

This quality of devotion and the rewards I get from it are worth far more than any stocks or bonds in my father's estate—and cannot be taken away at the marginal rate of 55 percent. Plus, I can pass it on to my son without any generation-skipping surcharge.

And he left something else of perhaps even greater value: a good name. Many people quarreled with my father's ideas about taxes or about when to balance the budget. He faced frequent opposition to his belief in a large defense budget. Of course, most of the people he knew disagreed with him about RN. But no one ever questioned that he came by his views honestly, by means of research and analysis and sometimes sentiment, but not for any venal reason or by the process of money changing hands. His reputation for honesty was simply without a speck of question upon it.

This good name cannot be taxed at all, at least not right now. My sister and I and our children will have it for as long as we keep it clean. It's priceless . . . incalculable in value.

So, in answer to the query from the forward high-school classmate, "Yes, my father did leave an immense estate, and yes, he did manage to beat the estate tax." The only problem is that I miss him every single minute, and I already had the best parts of the estate without his being gone, so the death part is pure loss.

Slate
10/25/1999

A City on a Hill, or a Looting Opportunity

JUST FOR MY OWN BAD SELF, I love living in the U.S.A. Every night when I go to sleep, I lie in bed next to my wonderful German shorthaired pointer, Brigid, and my Dalmatian, Susie, and I look out at the palm trees and the stars and think that the Gestapo isn't chasing me, and I am grateful. I think that the NKVD cannot come knocking on my door and send me to the Lubyanka, and I am ecstatic. I listen to my dogs' soft breathing, and I know my wifey is next door in her library with her four cats, reading, and I feel safe and grateful.

Living in America in 2006 for an upper-middle-class person like me, who, although overweight, still has decent health, is just paradise. There is no place like this place, a shining city on a hill, a gift from God every moment of every day.

But still, with all of that, something is seriously wrong. I could put it into statistics, and in a small way I will, but I'll mostly put it in layman's terms.

When I was a lad, the CEO of a major public company got paid about 30 or 40 times what the line worker got paid. Now, the figure is about 400 times. Why? What did they do in the executive suite to grow so great? Upon what meat do they feed? Why, as we are getting killed by foreign competition, do we need to pay our executives so much?

We have large corporations that paid their executives with stock options whose strike price was retroactively determined to be the lowest price of the quarter, so the options were "in the money" from day one. This largesse was not disclosed, which makes it straight-up fraud, and some of the executives have made billions from them (at least one has, at a large health-care company). Not one person involved has been charged with any crime, while young blacks who sell a tiny amount of drugs on a street corner do hard time. How can this be right?

We have immense corporations that cry the blues all day long about how their pension costs are killing them and they have to freeze pensions, or lay off workers, or end the pensions altogether (can you say "The Friendly

Skies"?) and turn the pension liabilities over to the tax-payers—and the same corporations set aside billions for the superpensions of the top executives. Even at my own dearly beloved General Motors, whose Cadillacs I love so much—precisely and exactly because I think of them being made by the sons and grandsons of men who fought in Vietnam and at Peleliu—there is severe action to get workers to quit and to lower their pensions. But at the same time at GM, spectacularly large executive-pension plans, totally unfunded, coming straight out of profits, keep retired top dogs happily playing golf at The Vintage (while the men who actually made the cars are saying, "Welcome to Wal-Mart, how can I help you?").

As I endlessly point out, for the rich, taxes are lower than they have ever been in my lifetime (to be fair, for the nonrich taxes are very low as well), while we accumulate government liabilities that will kill us in the long run. (And no, cutting spending will not work. Most federal and state spending is for items that are untouchable, like Medicare, education, military—and, most cruelly of all, interest on the national debt. Every President promises to cut spending, and none of them does it. None, unless a war comes to an end.)

We are mortgaging ourselves to foreigners on a scale that would make George Washington cry. Every day—every single day—we borrow a billion dollars from foreigners to buy petroleum from abroad, often from countries that hate us. We are the beggars of the world, financing our lavish lifestyle by selling our family heirlooms and by enslaving our progeny with the need to service the debt.

I don't see this—except for the taxes—as a GOP thing or a Democratic thing. It's just the way we live today. Drunken sailors from the Capitol to the freeways. Heirs living on their inheritance and spending it fast. The titans of corporate America getting as much as they can get away with and hiring lawyers and PR people if there is a problem. It is later than any dare think.

What I keep thinking is: Is this America, the America where the rich endlessly loot their stockholders and kick the employees in the teeth? Is this the America that our soldiers in Kirkuk and Anbar Province and Afghanistan are fighting for? Is this America, where we are going to wind up so far behind the financial eight ball, or that we won't be able to see because of mismanagement by both parties, the kind of America that our men and women in uniform are fighting for, losing limbs for, coming home in a box for?

On the Saturday before Memorial Day, I spoke at a gathering of widows and parents and children of men and women who had lost their loved ones in uniform in Iraq and Afghanistan. The woman who spoke before me was a beautiful, thin young woman named JoAnne Wrobleski, whose husband of less than two years—after four years' dating at Rutgers—had been killed in Iraq. She cried as she spoke, and she was right to cry, but she said she tried to keep love and trust in her heart. She spoke of her devotion to her country and her husband's pride in the flag. There was not a dry eye in the room, nor should there have been.

Are we keeping the faith with JoAnne Wrobleski? Are we keeping the faith with her husband? Are we maintaining an America that is not just a financial neighborhood, but also a brotherhood and a sisterhood worth losing your young husband for? Is this a community of the heart still, or just a looting opportunity? Will there even be a free America for JoAnne Wrobleski's descendants, or will we be a colony of the people to whom we have sold our soul? Are we keeping the faith with JoAnne Wrobleski? That is the question I ask about this beloved and glorious America for which Lieutenant Wrobleski died. If we are, we should be proud. If we are not, we had better change, and soon.

The New York Times
7/9/2006

I Never, Ever Experienced a True Miasma of Meaninglessness Until I Came Back to Hollywood

IT'S NOT DINNERTIME at Morton's. It's lunchtime. I am here with my posse from my new talk show. Over in the corner is Matt Damon, eating with someone who looks a lot like an agent. Near him is Alan Horn, the new head of Warner Bros. and one of the most capable (and kindest) human beings I have ever known.

My little group is puzzling over a meeting we had yesterday—or maybe it was last week—with an executive at a network. Let me tell you about it: Now, bear in mind that I, your humble servant, am the host of a cable-TV game show that's a big hit. Also bear in mind that ABC has started showing a super-successful show called *Who Wants to Be a Millionaire.* (No question mark, because everyone wants to be a millionaire unless, like Alan Horn, one is already *way* past millionaire.)

So, I had an idea for a game show that I would have on prime-time, network TV. Andrew Golder, the executive producer of my game show, came up with an incredibly brilliant add-on to my concept, and we took it to a production company about two months ago. The woman in charge said that if *Millionaire* worked, she would back us up in talking to the network. So, off we went to meet a woman exec at the net to pitch our game show.

She listened politely. Then she said she was "intrigued," always a word preceding trouble. Then she said probably the success of *Millionaire* would keep her net from buying any more quiz shows.

"Did I hear you right?" I asked. "You have evidence that quiz shows are the hit format of the millennium and you do not—repeat, *not*—want to make any more of them?"

"Well," she said, "yes, because we do not want to distract the viewers with more than one quiz show and confuse them."

"Wait a minute," I said. "Are you planning to show them both at the same time? Don't you only have one channel at a time? How can one take away from the other if only one is on at a time?"

"It still might be confusing," she said.

I took a deep breath. I looked around the familiar network surroundings. "You know," I said wearily, "I have been coming to meetings here for so many years—even decades. I used to come with a woman named Deane Barkley, who was once the highest-ranking woman in TV. She invented the made-for-TV movie. She used to say she had heard everything. I just wish she could have heard what you just said."

The network exec looked hurt. "I'm not saying we won't buy it," she said. "Definitely we're interested . . ."

Then a lot of polite talk, and then we left. So, now we're sitting at Morton's, and what I'm thinking is this: For six weeks, on and off, I was with my father in the surgical intensive care unit at the Washington Hospital Center, and I never once heard or saw anything that made me feel actually dizzy, actually vertiginous with confusion.

A family lost their 33-year-old son when he was hit by a truck while biking. They cried real tears. They hugged each other. They hugged me. They had me record a farewell speech for him to play at his graveside, because he had always been a joker and a funny guy, so one funny guy was saying farewell to another. That made sense.

I had an ancient African-American woman take my hand and say, "Mister Clear Eyes, will you say a prayer for me, and I'll say one for you and your daddy?"

I had nurses clean my father's backside after a bowel movement, refuse my offer of help, and smile and say they loved their jobs.

I made friends with a part of a real gang who were saying good-bye to a friend who had been in a blunt-trauma situation. That made sense.

I saw nurses push me out of the way as they rushed into a room to shove an endoscope down a man's throat so they could give him oxygen when he stopped breathing, and all the while, he fought them until they knocked him out with 8 mg of Versed—IV, stat!

I had dozens of men and women with sweet, unpretentious looks on their faces, wearing clothes from the Gap or Sears, ask how to spell my father's name, then tell me they would put my father in their prayer circles this Sunday. That made sense. And I have smelled disinfectant and fear and courage, but I never, ever experienced a true miasma of meaninglessness until I came back to Hollywood after he died.

Probably the woman who told me what she told me at the network was trying to do her best. I am sure her motives were good. But to have to live in this swamp, in this vortex of nonsense, year after year . . . where a vast amount of what happens every day just makes no sense at all. . . .

Oh, well. My pal Al keeps telling me it's better than the hospital, and in a way, it is. But in a way, for my 23 years here, I never really felt the falseness of Hollywood until I saw the reality of the ICU.

I ate my swordfish and made my reservations to go back to D.C. to deal with my father's estate.

Monday Night at Morton's
10/13/1999

BOSSES UNITE!
IT'S TIME TO
DEMAND THE
WORK YOUR
EMPLOYEES
OWE YOU

TRACI, A PART-TIME FILE CLERK and phone answerer, thinks that it's perfectly fine for her to begin work by taking an hour to make herself a tuna-fish casserole in my office kitchen, then talk to her friend Staci for half an hour. When she finally walks into the file room, she puts down a dangerously full glass of Diet Pepsi on top of the fax machine. She has already killed a typewriter that way.

Gail, my bookkeeper, believes in her heart that there is nothing wrong with routinely showing up a half hour late for work as long as she did not purposely intend to upset me.

Ray, the carpenter who attempts to keep the ramshackle house that I use as an office from falling down, believes that his work includes taking about ten minutes out of every hour to smoke cigarettes furiously and try to engage me in conversation while I am writing.

Rae, the graduate-school-educated researcher who tracks down bios of people involved in various Drexel Burnham exploits, turns in fine work, but only after she has told me in endless detail about her karate class and her latest love affair.

Nick and Dick, the men who prepare my car for its ventures on the Pacific Coast Highway, have yet to kill me. But they appear at the service station reeking of some strange combination of marijuana, sweat, and I don't want to know what else. I like to talk to them from about ten yards away.

It's no good saying that these are only the crazies who work for Ben Stein and that he should find better workers. These are the better workers. Others I have hired and fired are far worse.

Employees I see in other milieus are just as worrisome. At lawyers' offices, client meetings are routinely disturbed by rock music coming from a secretary's cubicle. At accountants' offices, calculations of tax liability are done by men and women listening to highly audible rap and heavy-metal music through headphones. And I am not talking just about loony California. My friends tell me about workers who will not work at airplane dealerships in Dallas, at law firms in Hartford, at publishing companies in Manhattan.

The employee who has no clue as to what he or she is doing there, who has only the dimmest notion of what he owes—while spouting encyclopedic knowledge about what is owed to him—is the national albatross.

Somehow, some extremely basic facts about what it means to work have been omitted from the American consciousness. The air is filled with talk about what we owe to employees—clean work spaces, decent wages, challenging work, nonsexist remarks—and that's just fine. But a few helpful hints about what the relationship between workers and employers is, or should be, are desperately needed.

I do not claim that what follows is the best that could be produced, but it's a start. Think of it as a Bill of Rights for Employers, or a Social Contract of the Workplace. Whatever you call it, we need it—or something like it—right now.

An Employer's Bill of Rights

1. PAYCHECKS MUST BE EARNED. Failure to work while being paid is theft from the employer. Workers voluntarily agree to perform certain duties, during set hours, at an

agreed-upon level of competence and care. In return, the employer promises to pay them money and other benefits.

If the worker fails to show up for work on time, leaves early, takes long lunches, comes back to work and talks on the phone all afternoon, paints her nails instead of filing, or talks to another worker instead of typing, that worker is breaking the terms of the contract with his or her employer.

In every sense, the worker who consistently fails to put in the hours he is getting paid for is stealing from his employer just as much as if the employer shortchanged the worker's paycheck.

2. TIME WASTED IN UNPRODUCTIVE ACTIVITIES, beyond an agreed-upon maximum, is time and money taken unethically from the employer.

The function of the workplace is to produce something: a car chassis, someone's income-tax return, a legal brief, an accounting of widgets, or an idea for a commercial for a laxative. It is not to provide amusement for the employees.

No one expects Stakhanovite ardor in postindustrial America. Some comfort at the work site is legitimate, and social intercourse is valuable. But to the extent that an employee considers his employment a vacation or time in day care, and considers his workplace a frat house or playpen, and behaves accordingly, he is stealing from his employer. His diversionary tactics may also be jeopardizing the employment of other employees, and by wasting the capital of the enterprise, he is cheating his colleagues as well as his employer.

3. WILLFUL FAILURE TO OBSERVE the rules of the workplace is a breach of a promise.

The conditions of work exist to facilitate the productivity of the enterprise. They have been agreed upon by employer and employee. Flouting them is as unethical a breach of duty by the employee as it would be for the employer arbitrarily to change the conditions of work for the employee by lengthening hours of work.

4. NURSING A GRIEVANCE is not an excuse to break the work contract unless the parties specifically agreed in advance that this should be the case.

Problems between worker and employer will come up frequently. They should be discussed. But to the extent that a worker takes offense at an employer's tone and strikes back by refusing to work productively that day, the worker is behaving wrongly. Certainly, the worker would be stunned if, in response to his own unpleasant tone, his employer refused to pay him for that day's work even if he performed satisfactorily. A grievance is one thing. Theft is another.

5. NOT BEING SUITED FOR A JOB is not an ethical reason for failing to do the job.

It is always possible, and often happens, that an employee is miscast in a certain role. In that case, he should resign or ask for reassignment. For him to continue in the unsuitable job and fail to perform his duties adequately is unethical.

6. TOOLS OF THE TRADE provided by the employer should be treated just like the boss's personal property. The things employees work with belong to other human beings. They are not floating unattached in thin air. To the extent that an employee abuses them, he is harming another's property just as if the employer capriciously vandalized the employees' cars in the company parking lot.

7. CLEANLINESS AND DECENT GROOMING are standards for the workplace. When the employee appears on the job sloppily dressed, and personally obnoxious to those around him, he is creating an unpleasant work situation just as if his employer refused to ventilate the room or allowed dirt to pile up on the office floor.

8. RELATIVE WEALTH IS NO EXCUSE for employee theft. Employees of large, wealthy employers routinely excuse their misconduct toward their bosses by saying, "Well, General Motors [or Ford or BBDO or Time Warner or the federal government] can afford it."

Obviously no productive and ethical civilization can exist if every person in it is allowed to steal from any person at all better off than the thief is. For one thing, there would be an unsolvable problem of computation. Unethical taking of time and money from an employer is taking from his family, from his wife, from his children, just as it would be if the employee broke into the employer's home and took his color TV.

Additionally, theft from the employer corporation is really theft from a large number of shareholders, many of whom are widows and orphans. Theft from an employer government is really theft from taxpayers, many of whom are poor. Stealing from the employer who "can afford it" is no less theft than stealing from an orphanage.

9. The "Others" in "Do unto Others" includes employers. Over time, people have devised schemes for getting along with one another. One is the notion of reciprocity. All humans should respect one another's name, bodily well-being, and property. These obligations are not eliminated when one person in a relationship happens to be an employer.

Business Month
April 1990

GRATITUDE

IT WAS TWO DAYS before Christmas. I was shopping with a friend in Beverly Hills. The sun was bright, and the temperature was almost perfect. As we turned a corner coming back from Dutton's bookstore, a real gem in Beverly Hills, we passed a manicure-and-pedicure shop. The door was wide open. As I looked in, I saw a woman in late middle age sprawled backward on a chair. She was having her foot massaged by a young Asian woman.

To me, the woman who was having the massage looked Jewish, although I might be wrong. I looked at her in her bliss and I thought, *I wonder if two generations ago her ancestors were selling bananas from a pushcart on Delancey Street on the Lower East Side, or if they were trembling at the approach of the pogrom in Lvov, or just what they were doing. And now she is basking in luxury on a sunny day in December in Beverly Hills. Glorious, glorious America. Glorious America.*

Then I thought, *What about the Vietnamese woman who is massaging her feet? It's not the job I would want, but it's probably a lot better job than whatever was likely to befall her in Vietnam. Probably a lot better than working in a rice paddy for barely starvation wages. She probably has a car and an apartment with air-conditioning and color TV, and most of all, she's free. Again, glorious America. Great, glorious America.*

And then we walked for a half hour among the crowds in Beverly Hills just to wait for some photos I had taken to be developed. There were Japanese, Russians, Iranians, ordinary Americans, all hustling and bustling about to buy whatever they wanted and needed for Christmas. Later, my friend bought an enormous piece of jewelry for his wife, and I waited while he waited for it, then watched him write an immense check for a diamond ring the size of a postage stamp.

And I thought, *America, America, God shed His grace on thee.* And then I thought of something else: None of this, absolutely none of it, would be there without the men and women of our armed forces. Every bit of what we have by virtue of being a free and prosperous nation, every ability to buy whatever book we want at Dutton's, every ability we have to come here from foreign lands and escape oppression, every speck of a chance we have to make it and become prosperous enough to have foot massages—all of this is behind the shield of the United States Army, Marines, Navy, Air Force, National Guard, and Reserves. Every speck of everything good we have by having full pantries and full stomachs is because someone fought and died for us at Bastogne or Tarawa. Every Jewish person like me or that woman getting her feet massaged owes our bare survival to the men and women who fought and won World War II. Hollywood didn't do it. The NBA didn't do it. Martha Stewart didn't do it. Donald Trump didn't do it. The U.S. Congress didn't do it. Men and women from places like Prescott, Arkansas, and Bedford, Virginia—people who we never heard of—they are the ones who did it.

And the freedom we live in, the truth that we did not succumb to Communism . . . that we owe also to the men and women who fought the cold war, in Korea and in Vietnam and in Europe and in Greenland. We owe them the very air of freedom we breathe.

Now, we do not have to fear an al-Qaeda that owns a whole country—Afghanistan—and can use it as a base to attack us. And this, too, is thanks to the men and women who liberated that sad country and tore al-Qaeda out of it.

Today and every day, men and women are fighting in Iraq in horrible conditions, with saboteurs and terrorists among them, to give that poor nation a chance to live in peace and democracy and to deny it as a haven for terrorism.

How much do we owe them? Far, far more than we can ever pay them. How much do we owe them for spending Christmas so far from their families, so far from safety, so far from comfort? How much do we owe men and women who offer up their very lives for total strangers like the people like me who were strolling up and down Beverly Drive?

Pay them more. Send their kids to school for free. Love them. Take them into our hearts. In the privacy of our homes—a privacy that their lives assured—be on our knees with gratitude to God that He sent such great souls into our lives. At this season of peace, all glory to the men and women who go to war far from home so we can indeed live and breathe and get our feet massaged and pray in peace. We are nothing, just zombies, without them.

The American Spectator Online
12/24/2004

A Voice as Big as America, and Just as Lonely

WHEN I THINK OF FRANK SINATRA, I think of a night at the Tropicana Hotel, the old one, in Las Vegas during the winter of 1975. I was there covering the apparent demise of Vegas in that recessed, high-gasoline-priced era. I was having dinner at the high-end restaurant at the Trop.

At the next table was a man eating by himself, with a corps of waiters and headwaiters gathered around him. It was the Chairman of the Board, ol' Blue Eyes himself—all alone in Vegas, and snow was falling on Tropicana Avenue.

But most of all, I think of another night about eight years ago. I was with a lively party at Morton's in Beverly Hills. It was late, and there was hardly anyone in the room. But Frank was there. Looking heavier, but still great. Walking slowly. With him was his wife, Barbara. There were also two bodyguards. Frank and Barbara didn't say one word to anyone the whole evening, including to each other. When they left with one bodyguard driving and one in the shotgun seat, they didn't even look up.

As I'm writing this, I'm looking at the jacket art for my favorite Sinatra disc. It's called, aptly enough, *No One Cares,* for the first song on the album. The art is from an LP released circa 1963. It features a party scene, showing women with early-'60s beehives and stoles talking to men in button-down shirts.

In the foreground is Frank, looking into a highball glass that's half-empty. One hand is on his cheek. The other is holding the glass. He's looking down at the drink and might as well be in Timbuktu for how isolated he is from everyone around him. He's in a crowd, but perfectly alone. He's even wearing a rumpled raincoat. Indoors.

Every song is about loneliness and loss: "I'll Never Smile Again," "Just Friends," "You Forgot All the Words." The picture goes perfectly with the songs, and the picture goes perfectly with that voice—that voice that's been around as long as 99 percent of Americans, that voice that's as much a part of the landscape as Times Square or Mount Rushmore or the beach at Santa Monica.

That voice—he used to be called "The Voice"—is the perfect American voice, because it embodies the one most basic American problem: loneliness. You can listen to Frank with Tommy Dorsey when he sang with Jo Stafford, in a haunting duet of "Stardust." Or you can listen to that voice when he sang his souped-up, electronically aided versions of "It Was a Very Good Year" and "The Last Dance." It's always the same sad, lonely voice. When he was a crooner singing above the voices of the screaming bobby-soxers at the Paramount before Pearl Harbor, his voice was far higher than it became. But it was still about weakness, vulnerability, loss.

You can hear it in his songs of the '50s and '60s: "Love and Marriage"—almost sung ironically in his case—and "Let's Fall in Love." The guy is all alone. It doesn't matter if he's friends with Sam Giancana and has his pick of the showgirls in Vegas. It doesn't even matter if he's hangin' with JFK and sharing the chicks with him and Sammy and Dean and Peter Lawford. This guy is, in his heart, all alone.

You really heard it as he got older and sang about doing it "his way." He did it his way because he was on the outside looking in. You can really hear it booming when he sings about the very good years, now past, and how his life has become just a few drops of vintage wine.

In 1990, that same night I saw Frank at Morton's, I had just bought a house on a cliff in Malibu. It was amazingly lonely there at night. No people, just distant waves and howls of coyotes and a mad wind through my palms and pines.

Night after night, my friend Betsy and I would listen to that wind, and then Betsy would say, "Put on Frank Sinatra with Tommy Dorsey. Put on that 'Call of the Canyon' song. It's like he was singing it for the people in this house."

And I would put it on, and high above the waves of the endless Pacific, with the wind roaring down on my little cabin, Betsy and I would dance the fox-trot to Frank Sinatra singing 50 years before. We were alone together. That lonely house, Betsy, Frank, and I.

I am going to miss that man. Bob Dylan connected for the first time in pop culture with the basic human feeling of anger. Frank connected as no one else ever has with an even more fundamental feeling: loneliness.

Frank alone in Morton's, alone in the Trop, alone in his songs: That's the Frank Sinatra we all could understand. That's the Frank who understood us.

The other Frank, the finger-snapping Rat Packer, was a publicist's figment. Frank alone, asking the bartender to set 'em up while he pretended he could do it his way, the lonely man whistling in the dark, that was the Frank we have lost and can't replace. The man was a star out of all proportion because he was one of us and could sing about it with a voice that came from you and me every night at 3 A.M.

E! Online
5/22/1998

SMALL WONDER DICTATORS FEAR HOLLYWOOD— IT CAN TAKE OVER THE BRAINS OF A CONTINENT

HA! IT IS MONDAY NIGHT, and I am actually at Morton's with Wifey. It is a balmy, lovely evening just after Thanksgiving, and I have a lot on my mind. My pal Barron has come over from Phoenix to have dinner with me. He also has a lot on his mind.

There is no one famous here except Alan and Marilyn Bergman, renowned lyricists of such movies as *The Way We Were;* and producer Steve Tisch, maker of films like *Forrest Gump;* and, with him, a great guy named Tom Arnold, star of the amazing Fox series *The Best Damn Sports Show Period.*

Tisch and Arnold recently had me as a guest, and tonight Tom greets me effusively. Steve greets me perfunctorily. He always seems to have a lot on his mind, too. Maybe that comes with being a billionaire's son.

Here is some of what I have on my mind: A few days ago, we took our son, Tommy, age 15, to see *Die Another Day*. We saw it in the most miserable theater in the world, one of the crappy little shoe boxes at the Beverly Center. Even so, the movie shone—a thrill a minute all the way through. No downtime at all—really a full-scale exercise of the human mind just to keep up with the action.

I loved Halle Berry, loved John Cleese, loved Judi Dench, loved like crazy the man who played the villain—whose name escapes me.

I had been bitching and moaning that the admission was $9, but once it started, it was magical. As I watched—in awe of the work and creativity it took to make those scenes on the ice and in the burning airplane in midair and on the swamp in North Korea—I had a thought that just has my little brain buzzing.

F. Scott Fitzgerald, the greatest American novelist, wrote in *Gatsby* how when the Dutch sailors first saw Long Island and then saw the great continent that rolled on behind Long Island Sound, they saw for the first time something commensurate in grandeur with the human imagination. What a brilliant concept.

Now, most of us will never discover a continent or fly in outer space to discover a star or a moon. Most of our lives are fairly humdrum. But the movies—not TV, but the movies—offer us something commensurate with the power of our imagination. The immensity of *Star Wars* or *Gone with the Wind* or *Blade Runner* or *Giant* or *Alien* is so vast, so breathtakingly beyond the ordinary, it manages to give us a sense of the vastness of creation itself.

In this way, a great movie—or a great canvas of a movie—is like faith or religion. It is a life-changing experience that shows us our potentialities. It gives us something to pattern our lives after. Small wonder the terrorist dictators fear Hollywood so much. Hollywood can take over the brains of a whole continent. Small wonder Khomeini called Western mass culture the Great Satan. It is really the great deliverer from small-mindedness.

Yes, a great movie is an undiscovered continent that we get to be the first in our brains to explore. And yet the people who make this glory are really in many ways fairly ordinary. They just happen to be plugged into something spectacular—the Hollywood fantasy-making apparatus. And what a difference that makes for all of us. What an amazing thing that a town exists mostly to make dreams—and sell them across the world.

Today at lunch, I ate with Bill Link and Al Burton. Link, along with his late partner Richard Levinson, created *Murder, She Wrote* and *Mannix* and *Columbo*. I do not for a minute compare these to *Star Wars* or *Gone with the Wind*, but these, too, were escapes and mind-enlarging journeys for maybe hundreds of millions of Americans. Al Burton helped to create *Mary Hartman, Mary Hartman* and a half-dozen Norman Lear sitcoms. He, as well, led viewers on voyages of discovery outside the humdrum. (He also invented *Win Ben Stein's Money,* and for that I am grateful.)

It occurred to me that Hollywood is really a port city. Here, we launch ships of the imagination into uncharted waters, and if they work, they take us with them. And I, by total chance, get to be a part of it.

We are launching probes far into the mind. We are a bustling port, with the shady characters of port cities but also with the possibilities for excitement and reward that ports have. I am excited just thinking about it.

As for Barron, he is thinking about a party for someone he loves. And I think I have an idea for a theme for it. Come as your favorite movie character, the guy or gal whom your imagination would let you be if you could be anyone.

As for me, I will come as a game-show host. Come on, everyone, come out here and join the party.

Next spaceship leaves anytime you want.

Monday Night at Morton's
12/4/2002

FATHER'S DAY
PERSPECTIVES

I AM ALL OVER MYSELF with self-pity here on this Father's Day. Our son is acting surly and rude and self-destructive. The last time I saw him, after he lifted a hundred bucks from me to go to a concert, he told me his goal in life was to live as far away from me as possible.

I don't think I am going to hear from him today. He's in western Massachusetts with his mom, my wife, and they are attending to getting him a summer job. We shall see. It is costing us so much more to have my wife there at a high-end hotel than Tommy can conceivably

earn—but I guess it's the discipline of work we're looking for. That would be a wonderful thing. He would get
more out of a feeling of having done a honest day's work
than he will out of a hundred years of psychotherapy.

Anyway, I am out at my house in Malibu. It is a gorgeous day. And here's what I am thinking:

First, how I wish my father were alive. I would trade
almost anything for just a few minutes with my father.
Just a few minutes of his smile and his thoughtfulness
and his love and his wisdom about my son and my life
and the world. Yesterday I listened for a long time to
my favorite CD, *Victory at Sea*. I love that disc because
when *Victory at Sea* came out 50 years ago, my pop and
I would sit on the couches in our basement, make a fire,
pop popcorn, and watch the Allies defeat the Axis powers. My father would comment on the points he knew
about from his service in the Navy and on the War Production Board, and then I would feel as if I had a special
insight no one else had. He was particularly saddened
by the losses in "strategic" daylight bombing, which, he
said, had not really done much good and had cost a lot
of lives. "The British got us into it because we were so
rich. They did the nighttime bombing and we did the
daytime, and the daytime got hit a lot harder."

I wish I remembered more of what he had said. I listened to that disc in bed and tears rolled down the side
of my face. Oh Pop, how I wish you were here.

In those days, the 1950s, all of our fathers had
served. My best pal, David Scull, had a father who was

(I think) an Army colonel (or maybe a major), and the Sculls had a photo of Mr. Scull in the Aleutians, if I remember it right—Kiska and Attu (which my spell-check does not know). He looked like a god. Everyone's father had gone away to war, and now they were back building a nation.

Now, only the very patriotic, the very young, the very brave serve. The rest of us sit at home and complain. (I wish I could send Senator Durbin into combat in Metz so he has a better idea of just who to call Nazis than he does now. I have always thought he was insane, and now he's making his own diagnosis. God help him.) The whole safety of the free world is defended by an infinitesimal band of men and women holding back the tide of barbarism.

What must their Father's Day be like? In a Humvee in al-Ramadi? Getting shot at? Getting attacked with IEDs? Wondering if they'll ever see tomorrow? Wondering if they'll ever see their kids again? Worried sick and having to pull all-day patrols?

And what must the Father's Day be like for their kids and their wives? Lonely, scared, terrified. And we are worrying here at home about interest rates, whether Google can stay as high as it is, and just when the housing boom will slow down. With our trivial worries, our self-pity, how can we even look at ourselves in the mirror?

And these fathers (and now mothers) who slumber at national cemeteries, who are having another day of grueling rehab at an army hospital in Germany or Walter

Reed: What can we, lost in our self-pity, possibly do or say or feel to thank them enough? What can we do for the Gold Star mothers and the fathers and the grand-parents of those killed in all of our wars? What about the hollow-eyed kids I remember from elementary school whose dads did not come home from Normandy or Iron Bottom Sound? What of Dawn Schissler, world's cutest carrottop, whose father died in training to make this country safe? I met her at the TAPS program over Memo-rial Day, and now I think of her about 50 times a day. She's about six. What can we do to make it up to her?

What can we do to remember them, to honor them? Nothing we can do can make it up to them, but we can carry love in our hearts all day and all night, day after day, and prayers for their safety, and thankfulness that this lush, ungrateful nation can still yield up so many heroes.

Nothing we can do can ever thank them enough though or make up for their pain. God bless them for all eternity. Time to get off the pity pot and down on my knees.

The American Spectator Online
6/20/2005

TO MY PARENTS, MORTON'S, WITH ITS RANKS OF BENTLEYS AND PORSCHES, WAS A MYSTERY OF PRETENSION

WELL, HERE I AM, back from Washington, D.C., with the producers and some of the writers of my new talk show, and we're going over questions and answers and last-minute guest switches.

There is a whole battalion of cute girls here, led by that woman who used to be married to Jim Carrey—oh, now what is her name?—she's really beautiful. Uhh . . . uhh . . . Lauren Holly. That's it. Not Lauryn Hill. Then there's Scott Sassa, the head of NBC, who's dining with someone named Oliver Platt, who is a fan of my show and apparently a huge actor.

Then there's Robin Popeil, the beautiful wife of Mr. Ron Popeil of Veg-O-Matic fame, and she just had a baby, so she's showing me the photo. The kid is gorgeous, which is what I would expect since she's so pretty. And then there's Kenny, the radio zillionaire, and his pals, who look a bit lugubrious tonight.

The wacky yet beautiful Dotty is not with them, and they look a bit lonely, to tell the truth. But they don't look as lonely as I feel. The reason I am back from Washington is that my father died last Wednesday, in a room at the intensive care unit of the Washington Hospital Center.

He's already been buried, because we Jews bury our dead right away. Plus, what with the Jewish New Year starting right away, there's no mourning any longer, and we're supposed to be going about our business.

My rabbi did say I was "allowed" to carry around my personal grief, however. He need not worry—I will.

I brought my father and my mother, who is now with him in eternity, to Morton's many a time. Years ago, I used to bring along Alan Horn, one of the finest men in town and now the head of Warner Bros. I think I brought them here with my pal Deanne Barkley on quite a few occasions. And I have a recollection of bringing them here with Michael Eisner a long time ago, too.

My parents were bewildered by Morton's. They were intellectuals, people who lived surrounded by videotapes of operas and ballets and books.

They did not care whether they had caviar or sword-fish or canned tuna and cereal. They just wanted to have their beloved books and their ideas and each other. They lived in extreme modesty even though they were famous and not poor.

To them, Morton's, with its ranks of Bentleys and Porsches and Mercedes, was a mystery of pretension without any apology. To them, a couple who owned a 20-year-old Chevrolet—which I imagine is crying for them in its lonely parking space at the Watergate, just as I am crying for them at Morton's—the idea of spending a hundred grand on a car was simply insane.

My father once told me he never knew anyone who ever had a mistress (at least he didn't think he did—he, in fact, definitely *did* know someone in that boat). To him, the older men with impossibly beautiful, huge-chested women who run back and forth to the bath-room to throw up and blow cocaine might as well have come down from Mars.

My father never in his life applied for a job. He never made a deal of any kind at all except to buy a house or write a book. To make a living by making deals for other people's labor, to get rich by it the way agents and pro-ducers do—that was beyond his imagining.

He knew it existed in theory—making money by bringing buyers and sellers together—but he could not fathom how men and women could live by pro-cessing others' labor, not actually producing anything themselves. When he saw them in their sleekness at

Morton's, he recoiled the way he would have from a hot radiator.

Noise. He could not stand loud noise. Why have it at Morton's and make the diners shout over it? Why not have peace and quiet and let people exchange their thoughts? That many of the diners might not have any thoughts beyond looking thin and having big breasts or counting money probably occurred to him the way a deadly snake would occur to him, so he did not think about it often.

My father did not really belong to this age or this place, my club, Morton's. Tonight, knowing my father's not on Earth to balance out its lewd allure, I feel alone. And frightened. It's as if the fog out on Melrose has settled inside for good.

There are more beautiful women here than I have seen for months, and Pop would not have gotten that either. A man had a wife, and that was it. Boom. The end. *Gar nicht.*

Well, I had better stop thinking about this. I have a show to do and people to meet and please and money to get and spend. My father was not realistic, and the people at Morton's are. That's the end of it. Except that my father just was always so damned clean, and I miss him so much sitting all alone in this fog.

Monday Night at Morton's
9/29/2000

NO MOVIE OR TV SHOW HOLLYWOOD EVER CREATED IS AS HAUNTING AS HOLLYWOOD ITSELF

TO BEGIN ON WHAT HAS BECOME a typical day for me, I was picked up bright and early yesterday morning by a driver for CLS limousine service. (It actually stands for "Charlie's Limousine Service.")

The man was taking me to the airport so I could fly to a faraway city for a speech. I have been giving a fair number of out-of-town speeches lately, and the trips all begin with a driver and a Lincoln Town Car polished to a high gloss.

The driver was a black man who told me a story as we wended our way to LAX.

He had grown up in a very small town in Mississippi. His father was a sharecropper. His grandfather had a medium-size farm on which he grew (what else?) cotton.

My driver, whose name is Major Black—not for a rank in the Army, but as a name—had worked with his sister helping to "chop" cotton as a lad and as a teenager on his grandfather's farm.

"It's hard work," the driver said. He told me about how the rows where the cotton grows get surrounded by weeds. The ground gets hard and dry. You have to go down the rows with a hoe trying to hack out the weeds.

Then giant insects attack you. And you get cut by the thorns of weeds and by sharp outcroppings of the cotton plant. And the day is long and hot and humid.

"But all day, as I did this work," Major Black explained, "I would think, *I am going to leave someday and make it to Hollywood,* and that kept me going."

In the fall in Mississippi, at about the time of the first freeze, he and his sister would pick cotton. Their fingers would get cut by the leaves next to the cotton boll.

The horrible bugs would attack them and crawl inside their shirts. But he would be able to persevere because he was thinking of how he would leave and come to Hollywood.

When he was out of high school, he did come to Hollywood. He played his guitar at clubs and joints, and then he joined a disco band that became popular in the '70s and never really died.

The band is called Rose Royce. Some of you may remember it from the great comedy *Car Wash*. Major Black was not in the band at its peak, but he is in it now when he is not driving.

And it's the fulfillment of his dreams. He has cut a few discs, one of which is an achingly touching tribute to his late father, who died only a few months ago. ("I feel as if I lost my road map," said Major Black about the loss of his dad . . . and I know the feeling.)

When the car arrived at the airport, Major Black said he would send me a disc, which he has done. And it's a fine song, well played and well sung. But what moved me most about his story is that Hollywood was the Promised Land for him and got him through the hard times.

And as I got on my plane to Boston, I suddenly had a revelation about Hollywood: No movie or TV show Hollywood ever created is as remarkable or as haunting in the memory of America as Hollywood itself.

Hollywood itself is Hollywood's grandest creation: the place where a kid like River Phoenix could live in his car when he got to town and become a megastar, only to die in tragedy.

The place where my former cohost could be doing catering, and a few years later make hundreds of thousands of dollars with her creativity.

The place where even multimillionaires like my pal P. are drawn from their respectable jobs in the groves of academe to find glory on the set.

The place I dreamed of as I sweltered on the subway in New York and became dizzy from the vile smells when we were stuck between stations. Yes, I had a great, super job, but the subway is not paradise, not the garden of apotheosis.

In all human history, was there ever a place where ordinary people could come and feel that they had a good shot at transforming themselves so thoroughly as they can and do in Hollywood?

I have seen it in my own life. I have seen it in every life of everyone close to me here, from Norman Lear to Bill Murray to Michael Ovitz: The ordinary become extraordinary.

Now, to be sure, there is a strain to becoming extraordinary if you really start to believe you are more than human and you go to war with mortality itself, and from that comes anguished looks on the face.

But if you can stay humble and at the same time realize you truly have been transformed, like the children of Israel coming out of Egypt into the land of milk and honey, you can feel the power of the place.

And for those who do not come, the dream still is out there. There are other great cities and towns, and incredibly kind and fine people in Canaan, New Hampshire; Berea, Ohio; and, above all, Holland, Michigan. But those are not the places of dreams.

Those are not the places you dream of as a giant caterpillar crawls up your chest while you sweat and chop cotton.

Hollywood is the place, and its availability as a place you can be transformed, as the metamorphosis spot here on Earth where dreams come true, that is what makes it a national treasure.

Yes, some of our movies—like *Gone with the Wind* and *Blade Runner*—and TV shows like *All in the Family* have changed life, but it is Hollywood itself, the cockpit of dreams, that is the Emerald City.

We who live here embroiled in struggles about money and status do not even know where we are until we leave. Or until we see it through the eyes of a man who grew up chopping cotton.

Monday Night at Morton's
4/24/2002

165

WHEN SCARCITY LEADS TO MADNESS

HADAMAR, GERMANY, is a small, pictur-esque town not far from the fabled medieval storybook town of Limburg, with its oddly Russian Orthodox, onion-domed cathedral. For many years before the advent of the Third Reich, it had housed a large church with a psychiatric hospital attached. When the Nazis took power, on the direct orders of the Führer, Hadamar's mission was changed. It became a T4, a euthanasia center. Persons with mental diseases; with retardation; with vaguely defined "antisocial tendencies," which could include being divorced too often, changing jobs too often, drinking too much, or, of course, being Jewish or "Negro" or Gypsy, were sent to Hadamar in buses with curtains over the windows.

Once there, they were perfunctorily examined by doctors and nurses, photographed, stripped, dressed in old army uniforms, and then taken down a grim flight of stairs I walked down a few weeks ago, into a waiting room, and then into a medium-sized room with large white ceramic tiles, still cool to the touch. About 80 human beings were jammed into this room, roughly 25 by 15 feet. The doors were locked tightly, and then a doctor (it was strictly ordered that only a medical doctor, usually a psychiatrist, was to do the job) would turn on a valve that would release lethal clouds of carbon monoxide into the room.

In 20 minutes, all of the victims were dead. Most were dragged out to be cremated. The crematoria ovens were running 24 hours a day for close to two years, from late September of 1939 to mid-1941, belching smoke over the pretty little town of Hadamar, not more than a few hundred yards from the room where the killings took place. A few select corpses were taken to a table where their skulls were sawed open and their brains removed, to be carefully sent to topflight German medical schools for examination.

I was shown around this ghastly place by a careful, articulate woman who is the curator there. She explained to me, in the course of many explanations, that while there was a racial-purity goal involved here, in the sense that the Nazis were trying to create an "Aryan utopia," as she put it, there was also a large issue of economics. (And Hitler thought of himself as not just a genius at science and military policy and diplomacy, but also at economics.)

As explained by Ms. George and documented by posters from the day, the Nazis believed thoroughly in Malthusian economics. That is, they believed there would inevitably be shortages of food. The available food could either be eaten by mentally retarded people, who supposedly tended to reproduce much faster than careful, prudent Aryans of good mental health, or by unemployed vagabonds, portrayed as weighing heavily on the shoulders of the German workingman. However, by what were described then as good, sensible Nazi economic policies, the "unfit" could be "controlled," and the available food could feed the blond gods and goddesses of the Thousand-Year Reich.

"This was their economics," the curator said, "and they believed in it as much as they believed in their science about race." (I am paraphrasing from memory, but it's darned close.)

Hadamar was closed in 1941 as a euthanasia center because of protests from a nearby Catholic bishop. Three of his priests were beheaded for passing out copies of his sermon. But then shortly thereafter, it was reopened for other nauseating killing purposes, one of which was to murder half-Jewish children who had one parent at a concentration camp and one at labor or at war. The half-Jewish child would then be in a ward of some kind and would, as Ms. George put it in Nazi terms, be "a useless eater."

Just like the mentally ill people, the divorcées, and the unemployed, this child would be consuming resources needed for good Aryans, and thus it was scientifically sensible to give them an overdose of barbiturates and kill them and bury them at the small graveyard near the mental hospital. Less "useless eaters," more food for the Reich. Exhausted forced laborers from Russia and from the Balkan States were also killed there for the same reasons. They were not Aryans, and they also were "useless eaters." (There are two Star of David gravestones in the cemetery, and the doors have to be kept locked to prevent vandalism of those simple markers by neo-Nazis.)

As I thought about this horror show and walked among the markers (where nearby Germans also take their dogs for walks), I wondered if we in America were unintentionally following any similarly horrifyingly mistaken economists. Is there some Thomas Malthus in our economic-policy-making world who is saying seemingly scientific theories that will eventually be used to take innocent life? Frankly, and this is a great credit to American economic policy, I could not think of any. Despite our many problems, especially stunning ones about misconduct by our corporate ruling class, we do not have any kind of doctrine that would say it was sensible to kill the innocent on economic grounds, at least not on a mass basis.

In fact, the great glory of America is that our economics has always been based on the idea that abundance is the natural order of things, interrupted only by the Great Depression, in which all kinds of crank Marxist and right-wing theories grew but soon died in the glow of mass prosperity. (And the trauma to America from the First World War was far smaller than to Germany—and besides, the Germans had major pseudoscientific race theories for long before April 20, 1889, when Hitler was brought into a world that did not deserve him.) If there is always plenty, there is plenty to go around. No one need be killed for others to survive handsomely.

But as I looked over a wall at the cemetery at Hadamar to the town, a chilling thought came over me: What if the good times don't last? What if the oil suddenly stops flowing? What about the overwhelming Medicare catastrophe that is bearing down on us? Medicare's foreseeable liabilities, discounted to present value, already exceed the total national wealth, by some measures. What about retirement? What happens when the boomers retire and their savings are not enough to support them and Social Security's cupboard is bare? What happens then? Whom do we turn upon? Where will the fury go if the days of abundance end? What if we shake the cornucopia some time around 2026 and it's empty?

We have not had to face genuine scarcity in North America since at least 1940. We have certainly never had a generational crisis like what is coming in Medicare. What will happen down the road? Frankly, I don't know. But the economics of Hadamar stand grimly as a reminder of what not to do. In the cemetery at Hadamar there is a stark obelisk on which is written, in German, "Man, respect mankind." And while we're at it, man, American man, and American woman, make some economic-policy plans so that days of fear and anger like the days when the crematoria at Hadamar were running around the clock will never offer even the slightest temptation at all as sensible economics.

The New York Times
9/17/2006

SUGGESTED SPEECH FOR A PRESIDENT

TIMES ARE VERY TOUGH IN IRAQ, and if I were still a speechwriter for the President, as I was for Mr. Nixon and Mr. Ford, this is what I would suggest he say:

My fellow Americans, I have some sobering news. It is my duty above all to protect the nation and to protect the Constitution. I sincerely believed I was doing that when I ordered the invasion of Iraq. I still believe that Saddam Hussein was the most dangerous man in the world.

But it is clear to me now that things are not working out well in Iraq. Despite the incredible competence, bravery, and sacrifice of our men and women on the ground there, Iraq is still a violent, largely out-of-control country. We may be making more terrorists than we destroy. The word *quagmire* comes to mind.

It is clear that changes must be made. I have this morning accepted Secretary of Defense Donald Rumsfeld's resignation with sincere thanks for his service to the nation. Despite his flaws, he is a great American. He will be replaced by a truly heroic American, Senator John McCain of Arizona.

I relied on the best minds I could access to make my decisions about Iraq. I prayed long and earnestly. Nonetheless, I made mistakes, and good men and women died and hard-earned tax money was lost. Fine young men and women are crippled and disabled. It is time for a change. Therefore, inspired by Secretary Baker and Senator Kean's fine unofficial committee, I am convening a national, bipartisan blue-ribbon commission composed of leading Democrats, Independents, and Republicans, civilian and military, to start meeting at once and give me a recommendation in one month as to what our Iraq policy should be. All options are on the table.

That is, I will consider all options, no matter how critical of my present policy.

I want to close with this thought: I am just a man. I have no miraculous powers. I have no special pipeline to God. Like all Presidents, from Jefferson and Lincoln onward, I make mistakes and sometimes good people die. I am deeply sorry. Now, as we reexamine our policy, I would ask that you all pray for us to make the right decision. I am in politics. I get criticized for a living. But let us all stand behind the brave men and women and their families who fight for this nation and give up their lives for us. May God continue to bless us all, and especially those who wear the uniform and their loved ones.

CBS News Sunday Morning
10/29/2006

ABOUT THE AUTHOR

BEN STEIN can be seen talking about finance on Fox TV news every week and writing about it regularly in *The New York Times* Sunday Business section. No wonder: Not only is he the son of the world-famous economist and government advisor Herbert Stein, but Ben is a respected economist in his own right. He received his B.A. with honors in economics from Columbia University in 1966, studied economics in the graduate school of economics at Yale while he earned his law degree there, and worked as an economist for the Department of Commerce.

Ben Stein is known to many as a movie and television personality, especially from *Ferris Bueller's Day Off* and from his long-running quiz show, *Win Ben Stein's Money*. But he has probably worked more in personal and corporate finance than anything else. He has written about finance for *Barron's* and *The Wall Street Journal* for decades. He was one of the chief busters of the junk-bond frauds of the 1980s, has been a longtime critic of corporate executives' self-dealing, and has written three self-help books about personal finance. He frequently travels the country speaking about finance in both serious and humorous ways, and is a regular contributor to the *CBS News Sunday Morning*.

Website: **www.benstein.com**